God's Vision
Our Mission

by

Ray Llarena

God's Vision, Our Mission
Copyright © 2024 by Ray Llarena

Published by:

McDougal Publishing
P.O. Box 3595
Hagerstown, MD 21742-3595

ISBN 978-1-58158-210-7

Printed on demand in the US, the UK, and Australia
For Worldwide Distribution

DEDICATION

To men and women everywhere who want God's vision to be their mission.

CONTENTS

**Declare His glory among the nations,
His wonders among all peoples.**
— 1 Chronicles 16:24, NKJV

**For so the Lord has commanded us:
"I have set you as a light to the Gentiles,
That you should be for salvation
to the ends of the earth."**
— Acts 13:47, NKJV

**That He would grant you, according to
the riches of His glory, to be strengthened
with might through His Spirit in the
inner man, that Christ may dwell in your
hearts through faith; that you, being
rooted and grounded in love, may be
able to comprehend with all the saints
what is the width and length and depth
and height—to know the love of Christ
which passes knowledge; that you may
be filled with all the fullness of God.**
— Ephesians 3:16-17, NKJV

FOREWORD BY HAROLD MCDOUGAL

The spring of 1996 was a very exciting time for all of us who knew Bishop Ray Llarena, for he had just made a serious move, accepting the pastorate of the forty-year-old Faith Tabernacle in downtown Chicago. Ray was only the fifth pastor to hold that position. But when he arrived, the church was in a very serious crisis. There was a financial debt of more than $1.8 million. The church had mortgaged the building, the parsonage, and a house at the back of the property they owned and rented to members, no payments had been made for many months, and the bank was looking for a way to foreclose on the property without angering the community.

Other matters had also not gone well recently for the church, and many of the faithful members were demoralized and looking to take their membership elsewhere. It was a critical moment for the church and also for Pastor Ray.

Those of us who knew him knew that he was up to the challenge. For many years we had watched as he took great leaps of faith in his personal life and in his ministry, and at every step, he had been blessed by God. When he tackled the challenge at Faith Tabernacle, we were not only standing behind him; we were certain that he would succeed.

His early services at the church were phenomenal and the immediate issues facing the church began to be corrected immediately. Attendance was up, giving was up, bills were being paid on time, a goal was set to pay off the $1.8 million mortgage within three years, and substantial pledges had come in toward that end. It was a promising start.

There were other problems. Faith Tabernacle had long been a missionary church, a giving church, but in recent years it had seemed to turn inward, and pledges of support for missionaries had gone unpaid. This troubled Pastor Ray. How could the church be blessed if it didn't keep its commitments?

To get the church moving again in the right direction, Pastor Ray was led to present a series of teachings in which he laid out very basically God's vision for His Church and for His people as individuals, and he challenged the people of Faith Tabernacle to make this vision their own. "God's vision," he declared, "must become our mission." The result was a series of teachings that are applicable to any Christian life and any Christian church in any location and in any time period. Therefore, we have compiled these teachings and presented them for the first time to the public at large, *God's Vision, Our Mission.*

Harold McDougal

CHAPTER 1

GOD HAS A VISION FOR US

Where there is no vision, the people perish: but he that keepeth the law, happy is he.   Proverbs 19:18

I believe God has a vision for His people. He has a dream, a purpose, a destiny for us—for each local church and for each individual believer. I also believe that we can enter into the fulfillment of that vision if we are willing to walk in obedience to the Lord our God.

A believer may seem to have a vital life in God. Such a one may be able to quote the Word. He may have the ability to express himself and his love for the Lord in worship. He may be quite happy and content in his local church. But is he attaining the goal that the Lord has for him?

Above and beyond the excitement, the clapping, the dancing, the rejoicing in the Lord, the singing and the shouting, what is it that God would really like to see accomplished in our lives? What do we ourselves want to accomplish? What goals do we have that we would like to reach, that we might say, "We have attained; we have fulfilled; we have accomplished; and we have done it to the glory of God"?

One thing is certain: Without a vision, we cannot move forward. If we do not know where we are going, we will be scattered in all directions, never reaching God's goal for us.

Paul reveals part of God's goal for us in his letter to the believers at Philippi:

... be found in him, not having mine own righteousness, which is of the law, but that which is through the faith of Christ, the righteousness which is of God by faith: that I may know him, and the power of his resurrection, and the fellowship of his sufferings, being made conformable unto his death; if by any means I might attain unto the resurrection of the dead. Not as though I had already attained, either were already perfect: but I follow after, if that I may apprehend that for which also I am apprehended of Christ Jesus. Brethren, I count not myself to have apprehended: but this one thing I do, forgetting those things which are behind, and reaching forth unto those things which are before, I press toward the mark for the prize of the high calling of God in Christ Jesus. Philippians 3:9-14

"Forgetting those things which are behind," "reaching forth unto those things which are before" ... this is what vision is all about! Too many believers live in the past. They spend their time looking back, regretting past mistakes and decisions. They look to past situations in which they were wronged, blaming circumstances for preventing them from becoming all that God intended. But such is not God's plan for us!

Whether you like it or not, God's ministry will move on. Whether you cooperate or not, God's work will advance. Whether you're going to be involved and committed or not, the Kingdom of God will progress. The Church will move straight ahead according to God's schedule.

There is a widespread mentality in the Church today that says, "Oh, look at what is happening! The Church is being overshadowed by the sin of the world. Things are getting worse and worse all the time. We can never overcome, because the kingdom of darkness is growing stronger and stronger upon the earth." We hear these things, but are they true? What does the Bible say?

> *For unto us a child is born, unto us a son is given: and the government shall be upon his shoulder: and his name shall be called Wonderful, Counsellor, The mighty God, The everlasting Father, The Prince of Peace. Of the increase of his government and peace there shall be no end, upon the throne of David, and upon his kingdom, to order it, and to establish it with judgment and with justice from henceforth even for ever. The zeal of the LORD of hosts will perform this.* Isaiah 9:6-7

There is no question that this Child was the Lamb, Christ Jesus. And what do we read concerning His Kingdom? *"Of the increase of his government there shall be no end."* Since its inception upon the earth, the government of Christ has been increasing, not diminishing. Think about it. Jesus began with just twelve men. Now there are millions of believers. Does that sound to you like a Church that is being overtaken by darkness? No!

God's Kingdom, His purposes, will continue to move forward in the earth. God will continue to do His work in men's hearts and lives. And we can choose either to be a part of it or not. Ministry moves forward because of our determination to do God's work. God has a purpose for each one of us, He has a purpose for each local church that He has established, and He has a purpose for the corporate Church.

But on any of these levels, we can only move forward when we determine in our hearts that we will work to accomplish God's purpose and plan. We will not accomplish anything by sitting down and saying, "Oh, others are doing the work of the ministry, so I don't need to do it." God's purposes for us will only be realized if each of us has determined that he will be involved, he will participate, he will help to carry the load, and he will see the vision accomplished.

We began this chapter with a Scripture from the book of Proverbs. Let's read it again:

Where there is no vision, the people perish: but he that keepeth the law, happy is he. Proverbs 19:18

When there is no vision, when there is no call, there can be no accomplishment. Without a vision, there is no real sense of purpose. When there is no vision, there is no manifestation of reward for your efforts, time, energy, and finances. So, without a vision, there is no real reason to move forward, and so there is no growth, no pressing on. Without a vision, we will miss God. In others words, the people will perish.

You may have a vision for your life. Perhaps your vision is that you want to get married. Perhaps you are pursuing a course of study so that you may have a career or so that you may advance in your career. Whatever your vision, it is up to you to work toward making it happen. There will be sacrifices required. Is your vision worth the cost?

If you are just drifting through life, enjoying whatever comes to you, then you will never reach your goal because you do not have one. You will not become what God intends you to be, and you will not see the ministry that He has for you.

But if there is a vision, it will be a very different story. If you have a vision, you have a reason to face the struggles. There is a sense of purpose in your life and in your striving. You overcome difficulties in order to attain your goal.

Why is vision so important? I believe there are three reasons we should embrace a vision of what God wants to do in us and through us:

First, vision provides a sense of purpose. Without that sense of purpose, we just float along, going from place to place, but without a destination. We waste our energy, our time, and our money. But if we have a vision, then we have purpose, and our purpose is to see that vision fulfilled in our lives and in the life of the church. If we have a vision, then every moment counts toward the fulfillment and the attainment of that vision. The enemy may rise up against us, but if we have a vision and a purpose, then we can be determined to fight him and to do the work of God, to carry out His purposes.

Second, vision gives us clarity of direction. It is good to have an idea, but it is better to have a plan. We need a sense of direction in our lives. Why begin a trip if we have no idea of our destination? We will only waste our time, energy, and resources if we run around with no destination in mind. A vision—for a church or for an individual—will provide clarity of direction. The ultimate direction is to find ourselves complete in God, conformed to the image of Christ. All other goals along the way will be taking us in that same direction.

Third, vision gives us the courage to accomplish great things. When there is something important that you would like to attain, you will sacrifice everything and stand against anything that hinders you from striving to meet that goal. You will be willing to say no to the flesh, you will be willing to face inconvenience, you will be willing to lay down everything on the altar for the purpose of seeing what you desire, what you dream of, come to pass. When you have purposed in your heart to carry out your vision, God will give you the courage and the boldness to do it. As you do so, you will grow in courage to do the work of God.

Finally, vision gives a sense of responsibility. The responsibility of the vision lies with the one who has the burden of the vision.

Some of the most disorganized and irresponsible people I know are Christians. They take their liberty for license. Such people love to quote John 8:36: *"If the Son therefore shall make you free, ye shall be free indeed,"* and they say. "I'm free!" But we need to be responsible people. When God gives us a task, we need to be faithful to complete it. We need to be in a position of accountability toward each other and toward God.

If we are to accomplish what God has for us, we need to have a vision. We need to find His purpose, to sense His direction, to take upon ourselves His courage, His strength, and His power; and then we need to be responsible enough to participate in that vision and carry it out to fulfillment.

So we see that vision is important; it is crucial if we are not to become stagnant in our walk with God. But there are many kinds of visions or goals. Some are worthy, and some are not. Some are worth sacrificing for, and others are not. So what should our vision be?

Let's look at it another way: What is God's vision for the Church? If we believe that He has an overreaching purpose for the Church, it is not too far-fetched to believe also that He wants us to know what that purpose is. How else are we to know what to work toward?

I believe that, not only does God have a goal for us, several goals in fact, but He has clearly stated them in His Word.

The first of these we have already touched upon:

For whom he did foreknow, he also did predestinate to be conformed to the image of his Son, that he might be the firstborn among many brethren.   Romans 8:29

The goal for each one of us is the same: we are to be conformed to Christ's image. While there are different giftings, different abilities, different facets of Christ to shine through each of us, we are all to come to that place of conformity. This is the basic underlying vision that we can all carry within our hearts—the vision of Christ. None who are called by His name can have any other goal before this, and all of our goals should contribute to this one.

But is that all that we are to strive for? In one sense, yes. Everything we reach for brings us closer to this goal. But we are by no means to be morbidly introspective, continually looking inward to gauge our progress. We become like Jesus as we do what He directs.

We can look to the words of Christ Himself if we want to find His heart for us. Just before He ascended to Heaven, He told His disciples:

Go ye therefore, and teach all nations, baptizing them in the name of the Father, and of the Son, and of the Holy Ghost: teaching them to observe all things whatsoever I have commanded you: and, lo, I am with you alway, even unto the end of the world. Amen.

Matthew 28:19-20

God's heart for us is to have His heart for others.
Peter wrote:

The LORD is not slack concerning his promise, as some men count slackness; but is longsuffering to us-ward, not willing that any should perish, but that all should come to repentance.

2 Peter 3:9

This is God's vision! This is why He sent His Son, Jesus. The vision of the Father became the vision of the Son.

We must become a soul-winning Church. If there is one thing that is close to the heart of God, it is the winning of the lost. We are to seek them, not to condemn them, not to punish them, not to harass them, but to present to them the love of God, the grace of God, and the mercy of God. We are to tell them there is an alternative. Jesus made a way for them to know God.

The Church in this day needs to be consumed with winning souls. If there is only one thing that is precious in the sight of God, it is souls. More than parking lots, more than buildings, more than bank accounts souls are the riches of churches today. Why do so many churches have empty seats? Why are they not filled to overflowing? Because the Church as a whole has no vision for souls. We have no vision for eternity. We have no vision for those who are dying without Christ.

*For the Son of man is come to seek and to save that which was
lost.*   Luke 19:10

Let us be consumed with the passion of Jesus Christ for the souls of men.

How can we reach that goal? Each one must reach one. Each one of us must shine for Jesus Christ. We live in a dying world where souls are literally going to Hell. Many need to be brought into the Kingdom of God before it is too late.

We can sing and clap and shout, and that is wonderful. We can put something in the offering plate. We may even shed a tear or two and feel that we have done what we can for the glory of the Lord. But we need to ask ourselves some questions:

- How many souls have I brought into the Kingdom of God?
- How many lives have I influenced for Jesus Christ?
- How many hearts have I touched recently for God?

Jesus instructed His disciples:

*And as ye go, preach, saying, The kingdom of heaven is at hand.
Heal the sick, cleanse the lepers, raise the dead, cast out devils:
freely ye have received, freely give.*   Matthew 10:7-8

We have received freely, and freely we must give. Give life, give light, give Jesus so that the broken may find wholeness, that the outcasts may find acceptance, that the blind may see, that those who are oppressed may be delivered, and that those who walk in death may know life.

That is our vision, beloved, winning souls for Jesus Christ. This should be our first priority. We are each a testimony, an epistle being read by others. What does your life say? Does your life match your profession of faith? We are to shine like a light for Christ. Allow the Lord to ignite a passion for lost souls within you — for the souls of loved ones, of friends, of those the Lord brings your way.

Have you shared your faith with anyone lately? If each believer would just reach out to one person, if each one would bring one nonbeliever to church, the churches would soon be overflowing. That's the kind of problem we would love to see!

Secondly, we need praying churches. I am not speaking of a handful of people coming together in formal church settings once a week. Wherever you live, you should be a powerhouse of prayer. Pray that the supernatural power of God be demonstrated, that the anointing of God be revealed, that your life becomes a prayer in itself, that people would see the power of the Lord in you. Prayer is declaring your trust and faith in God to do the impossible.

All too often, those who are continually asking for prayer are not praying themselves. Why not? Because they don't know how to pray. But if you don't know how to pray, you don't need to read a book about prayer, hear a teaching about prayer, or have a counseling session concerning prayer. You need to go to the Source of prayer, Jesus Christ. It is He who has said, "Pray this way" (see Matthew 6:9 and Luke 11:2). When you come to Him, He will teach you how to pray and what to pray. I am not against teachings and studies, but the only way to learn how to pray is to pray.

When I was a new believer, I had a friend who would always pray for me. And whenever he prayed for me, there were results. But there came a time when I was in a place of great need, and my friend was not there. I could not ask him to pray for me, so I had no one to turn to. That's when I began to experience prayer for myself. That is when I learned to cry out to God, and I learned that God heard my prayers and was no respecter of persons in regards to prayer.

From that time on, I have been developing that communication and communion with God. I have learned to touch the throne of God, to reach out to Him. I have learned to come into the very presence of God. And I have experienced the power of prayer!

Just imagine what would happen if every believer in every church began to truly pray! The power of God can be ministered, manifested, and demonstrated when we truly learn how to pray. This is not simply mumbling and rumbling some words. Real prayer happens when our hearts are in tune with God and our spirits are reaching out to Him. He who is a stranger to prayer is a stranger to the power of God, but he who loves to pray knows God's power. He who is not a person of prayer is not an overcomer, but he who is a prayerful person is a victorious person.

Learn to pray! Don't panic when problems arise. Know that there is a power behind you—the power of prayer. Don't feel sorry for yourself when you are going through difficulties. Exercise the privilege given to you to pray. Church, it is about time for us to understand that prayer works! God is faithful, and He will hear our prayers. Prayer is an opportunity for God's power to flow and minister to His people.

Prayer must become an integral part of our lives. It was not intended to be reserved for grace before meals or for bedtime. Prayer is a gift, a privilege granted to us by Almighty God. It is our time to commune with Him, to fellowship with Him.

Thirdly, we must have a vision for true worship. The highest expression of our faith is worship. Praise and worship are very important, but they do not consist merely of singing a few songs. Worship is standing in the presence of God, waiting for His voice to speak. It is allowing Him to speak into our hearts, our minds, our attitudes, and our spirits. True worship transforms us, changing our hearts, because when we truly worship, we have come into the presence of the Lord. Real worship changes our position in life, and it changes our viewpoint. No matter how glorious a time of worship may seem, if you have not been transformed, then you have not yet worshiped the Lord *"in spirit and in truth"* (John 4:23-24).

Beloved, we need to learn how to enter into the presence of God. We need to learn to discipline ourselves to wait in His presence. We need to educate ourselves concerning how to be in tune with God. We need to worship God *"in spirit and in truth."* I believe that if every Christian learned to worship God, the counseling rooms in the churches would be empty, and most of our problems would be solved by His presence. Healings would occur, as people entered into worship to God. We will find the wholeness we seek if we humble ourselves to truly worship the Lord. We need to be a people of worship. We need to bring the glory of God to the earth. But it can only be done when God's people truly worship Him.

Worship is a matter of the heart. We really don't need music, and we don't need singing. We don't need to be in a local church building or in the presence of other believers. We are the Church. You are the Church, and I am the Church. The object of our worship is within us, not in a building. Let us determine in our hearts that we will worship God *"in spirit and in truth."*

When the Church begins to walk in worship, carrying the presence of the Lord, then the anointing and the power of God will flow like a mighty flood. It will flow in every direction and will bring salvation to many.

Church, we need to live a life that reflects the glory of the Lord. We need to be those who carry the presence of the Lord with us wherever we go, bearing the message of salvation, praying as we go and allowing our lives to be one of worship to our God. Our integrity, our honesty, our sincerity, our purity, and our faithfulness are more important than our own selfish ways. After all, our ways will never accomplish the purposes of God for our lives.

Let us draw near to the Lord Jesus Christ, who is our example of true soul-winning, of an effective prayer life, and of worship. That is our vision, and that is our hope.

Beloved, now are we the sons of God, and it doth not yet appear what we shall be: but we know that, when he shall appear, we shall be like him; for we shall see him as he is. And every man that hath this hope in him purifieth himself, even as he is pure.

1 John 3:2-3

CHAPTER 2

GOD'S VISION FOR SOULS

And the LORD answered me, and said, Write the vision, and make it plain upon tables, that he may run that readeth it.

Habakkuk 2:2

It is one thing to have a vision, but it is quite another thing to see that vision come to pass. A vision is worthless unless it is carried out. When God grants us a vision, it is not so that others can look at it and see how wonderful it is. When God imparts His purposes to us, it is so that we will be actively involved in helping those purposes to be accomplished on the earth. We are to *"make it plain"* — to make it understandable. Then we and all those who lay hold of that vision, or "see" the vision, can run with it.

As the people of God, we have a purpose, for God has a vision, and that vision must become our vision. This was the foundation of Christ's mission when He walked the earth. And now, God's vision, Christ's mission, has been passed to us. It is now our vision, and our vision will direct us and help us to focus upon our destiny in God. As we work together toward our common destiny, we will find unity of purpose in Him.

I believe the first part of God's vision for the Church today is that we should be a soul-winning Church. This is not just for those who count themselves evangelists, nor is it only for those congregations that already have a vision for the lost. The Lord's vision for His Church is that we become people with a passion for souls and a burning desire to reach sinners. He wants each one of us to be among those who reach out to the lost.

We are to win people to Christ, and in order to do that, we must have compassion and concern for the sinner. Think about it. It isn't right for us to enjoy the blessing, anointing, and fellowship of God while there are so many who are in the hands of the devil. It's not fair! And it isn't what God has in mind for His people either.

Jesus said:

For God so loved the world, that he gave his only begotten Son, that whosoever believeth in him should not perish, but have everlasting life. For God sent not his Son into the world to condemn the world; but that the world through him might be saved.

John 3:16-17

Jesus was sent to this world with a purpose. His mission was the vision of God. What is that vision? That none should perish, but that all should come to repentance and life in Him. God loves the world, and that includes everyone in it. He sees the world dying in sin, on its way to Hell, but He does not want any to perish—not the alcoholic, not the homosexual, not the prostitute, not the drug addict, the criminal, the thief, or the liar. His Word is clear:

The Lord is not slack concerning his promise, as some men count slackness; but is longsuffering to us-ward, not willing that any should perish, but that all should come to repentance.

2 Peter 3:9

God is *"not willing that any should perish."* He wants all to repent. That is the vision of God! That is why there had to be a cross. Christ came to fulfill a mission, and He embraced the vision of the Father. It became His mission, even to His death on the cross of Calvary. Why? Because God is *"not willing that any should perish."*

The salvation of souls is the very heartbeat of God. Christ spoke of this mission to His disciples:

> *Therefore said he unto them, The harvest truly is great, but the labourers are few: pray ye therefore the Lord of the harvest, that he would send forth labourers into his harvest. Go your ways: behold, I send you forth as lambs among wolves.* Luke 10:2-3

Please notice something about these verses. The disciples were told to pray for workers (verse 2), but that was not all they were to do. The next verse gives them further direction: *"Go ... I send you ... "* This reminds me of the prophet Isaiah, a man with a heart for God. Do you recall his prayer?

> *Also I heard the voice of the LORD, saying, Whom shall I send, and who will go for us? Then said I, Here am I; send me. And he said, Go, and tell this people ... .*   Isaiah 6:8-9

Can we be as Isaiah? May you be among those who will pray, "Lord, here am I; send me. Send me forth to bring in the harvest and to reap the grain. Send me forth, Lord, to touch lives and to be a blessing. Send me forth, Lord, to be the light of the world. Help me to shine for You," and then do it!

Paul wrote:

*For I am not ashamed of the gospel of Christ: for it is the power
of God unto salvation to every one that believeth; to the Jew first,
and also to the Greek.*   Romans 1:16

Like Paul, you should not be ashamed of your salvation. You
should not be ashamed of your relationship with Jesus Christ. You
should not be ashamed that you are a child of God. You should not
be ashamed that you are a follower of Jesus Christ or that you are
His disciple. There is no shame in any of these things, but rather
great joy and beauty! You should be proud that eternal life dwells
within you. You should be proud that you carry the hope of glory.
The world needs to see that. They need to hear that. The world is
longing to experience what you have.

The Gospel of Christ is the power of God unto salvation. It can
transform lives. It can change people's destinies. It will change
the course of life for every person who responds to it. We need to
hear the truth of the Gospel.

God's Word presents us with the reality of the cross, the incar-
nation, and the resurrection of Jesus Christ for this very reason.
We see that He was born, lived on the earth, was crucified, and
resurrected for one purpose: that the shackles of sin might be
broken, so that men and women might enter into the Kingdom of
God and know eternal life in Him.

Church, we had better align ourselves with God's vision. We had
better lay hold of Christ's mission: the winning of souls. We know
that men need to believe, but Paul asked some hard questions:

*For whosoever shall call upon the name of the Lord shall be saved.
How then shall they call on him in whom they have not believed?*

and how shall they believe in him of whom they have not heard?
and how shall they hear without a preacher? And how shall they
preach, except they be sent? as it is written, How beautiful are
the feet of them that preach the gospel of peace, and bring glad
tidings of good things! Romans 10:13-15

"How shall they believe in him of whom they have not heard?" How
can they hear unless someone tells them? You who are enjoying
salvation and the blessing of God, you who are filled with the Holy
Spirit and are glad in the Lord, did someone reach out to you with
the Good News about Christ? Did someone go out of his way to
bring you to the Lord? Did someone witness to you, minister to
you, pray for you, shine the light of God into your life? Someone,
somewhere, at some time, planted the seed of the Gospel in you.
How can you do less for others?

The salvation of souls is the heartbeat of God. You see, Hell was
not created for man; it was created for the devil and his angels:

Then shall he say also unto them on the left hand, Depart from
me, ye cursed, into everlasting fire, prepared for the devil and his
angels ... . Matthew 25:41

Sinners are not going to Hell because of their sin; they will go
to Hell because they have not received the gift of eternal life. Why
haven't they received it? Often it is because no one has told them
about it. Yet the Church—which is to say, each one of us who
makes up that body—has been made accountable to spread the
Word and to show forth the life of Jesus Christ. We know that we
are all guilty of sin, that we have all fallen short (see Romans 3:23).

Everyone is under the guilt of sin and its condemnation. But, thank God, the Lord had a vision for His people. He envisioned a mighty army arising in the latter days to be a testimony to the glory of His name. He envisioned a people who would draw others into the Kingdom, so that its increase would know no end. He envisioned a people who would show forth His glory and His character. He envisioned the Church!

What if God had not entertained such a vision? What would it be like if God had not envisioned such a people? We know that all have sinned and come short of the glory of God (see Romans 3:23). We know also that the wages of sin is death (see Romans 6:23). The payoff, the consequence, the result of sin is death—a spiritual death, a separation from God. No matter what you may have heard preached, there is condemnation and judgment, and the wrath of God is real. These have not been abolished. We are all guilty. Therefore every one of us would have died because of our sin.

Beloved, remember this: you don't need to tell a sinner that he is a sinner. If he is a sinner, he knows it. What he needs is someone who will tell him how to escape from his sin. He already knows the diagnosis. He needs the remedy, the cure for his sin. He needs to know what he can do to escape death.

Yes, the wages of sin is death; but thank God the scripture does not end there!

> *For the wages of sin is death; but the gift of God is eternal life through Jesus Christ our Lord.*   Romans 6:23

There is a beautiful word in this passage, and that word is *but*. *"But the gift of God ..."* By the grace of God, this verse of scripture does not end with death; it ends with life! God is offering us His gift of eternal life. You have received it, you have tasted it, you have experienced it, and you have been set free, transformed by the power of God. What is this eternal life? Is it something we will know only after we have died, or after the Lord has received us on the last day? The Word gives us a beautiful definition:

> *And this is life eternal, that they might know thee the only true God, and Jesus Christ, whom thou hast sent.*   John 17:3

The gift of God is eternal life through Jesus Christ. It is our privilege to be a part of God's plan to impart His life to many — to all the world. People will never see the glory of God unless they are born into God's Kingdom. Those who are in sin will only reap sin's rewards, unless someone reaches out to them with the Good News of the Gospel.

Still, Christians have many excuses: "Pastor, I'm struggling myself." Do you know why you're struggling? Because you are so focused on yourself. Turn your thoughts to the needs of others. If you do that, you will find yourself with a different outlook on life. Look to the need of others for salvation.

"I wouldn't know what to say." Then dig into the Bible. Pray. Be filled up with the life of the Lord so that it will flow freely from you, and you can draw from the treasures of the Word.

> *He that believeth on me, as the scripture hath said, out of his belly shall flow rivers of living water.*   John 7:38

Then said he unto them, Therefore every scribe which is instructed unto the kingdom of heaven is like unto a man that is an house-holder, which bringeth forth out of his treasure things new and old.   Matthew 13:52

Many believers fear rejection if they witness to others, but there are worse things than the rejection of man:

Whosoever therefore shall confess me before men, him will I confess also before my Father which is in heaven. But whosoever shall deny me before men, him will I also deny before my Father which is in heaven.   Matthew 10:32-33

If the Lord is preparing the way, and if we have sown the path with prayer, then we needn't worry about how we will be received. After all, if someone does not receive the message we bring, then they're not really rejecting us; they're rejecting the Lord we represent. Surely our concern for the sinner should far outweigh our concern for our own feelings!

Why should we be concerned about the lost? First, we have all been in their place. We were once sinners, so we know what it is like to be under condemnation and guilt. We know how it feels to fear judgment. We know how it is to walk in darkness, to be in bondage to sin. You have been there, and now you know what a great difference it makes to be in Christ! You have experienced what it is like to be released from the prison of sin and from the strongholds of the enemy. You have experienced the passage from death unto life. You were once dead, but now you have been resurrected; once lost, you have been found. You are enjoying the blessing of being in the presence of the Lord. But what of those who are still lost? It is our responsibility to reach out to them.

You are not a believer right now because you suddenly decided to be a Christian. Someone, at some point, invested time and energy in you. They showed you, they taught you, they prayed for you, they ministered to you. Perhaps they even hounded you. But finally the Gospel of Christ penetrated your heart and your spirit. The fire kept building until you melted in the presence of God, saying, "I'm a sinner! Come into my life, please, Lord Jesus."

We need to look to our roots in God, we need to look to our experiences in coming to Christ, and we need to minister with that same fire and excitement. We have been there, so we know what it is like to be forgiven and can help others come to that experience as well.

A second reason we need to care for the lost is that we are to be about our Father's business, as Jesus was. We need to heed the commands of the Word. We have seen the command of Christ that we pray for laborers. We also see this command to minister elsewhere:

> *But ye shall receive power, after that the Holy Ghost is come upon you: and ye shall be witnesses unto me both in Jerusalem, and in all Judaea, and in Samaria, and unto the uttermost part of the earth.*   Acts 1:8

Witnessing is Christ's command to the Church. Proclaim the truth. Testify to the fact that He is the Savior. Spread the message throughout the earth.

And he called his ten servants, and delivered them ten pounds, and said unto them, Occupy till I come.   Luke 19:13

Christ has left us and gone on to Heaven, but He left us with this command: *"Occupy till I come."* In other words, "Continue the work that I have begun until I return. I am leaving you behind for now, but I am sending the Comforter, the Holy Spirit, to you. So go out and preach the Gospel. Win the lost, deliver the sick and the oppressed. Bring them out from their bondage and set them free."

What are we to be occupied with? Reaching out to the souls of men, expanding the territory of God's Kingdom, destroying the strongholds of the enemy in people's lives.

Many believers are simply too lazy. They are content to enjoy the presence of God. The say, "Bless me, Lord. I love You, Lord. I want to serve You, Lord."

I hear the Lord saying, "You want to serve Me? All right. Will you go out to win the lost?"

"I'm sorry, Lord. I'm not an evangelist. That's not my gifting."

And so the command goes unanswered. I believe that the reason the devil is having such a good time here on the earth is that Christians are not occupying as they should. Instead, they are allowing the devil to occupy their territory. And not only does he occupy; he loves to conquer, to subdue, to overthrow, overpower, and rule.

"Occupy till I come." When Christ returns, I hope He will find you working, occupying for Him. Jesus said:

Follow me, and I will make you fishers of men.

Matthew 4:19

In military service, the very first thing recruits are taught is to follow orders. If they don't, there are consequences. It might be a hundred push-ups, it might be KP duty, it might be scrubbing a floor on your hands and knees. The reason the recruits follow orders is that they respect the one who has the stripes. It doesn't matter whether he is rich or poor, handsome or ugly, educated or not. He's the sergeant, and you had better listen to what he says. The sergeant is in control. If you follow and obey, you'll be in good shape.

Jesus is our Master. He is the King of Kings and the Lord of Lords. Our responsibility is to follow Him and to obey His orders. Disobedience to God is a sin. We may think that we can get away with less, that we can rely on the mercy of the Lord, but God's kindness does not detract from His vision. And He has a vision for souls. We have no option, beloved. We have orders to follow.

Winning the lost is not the job of a handful of people who are called to outreach ministry; it is the responsibility and the ministry of every born-again believer. We are all called to be fishers of men. Obviously, not too many fishermen just sit by the shore saying, "Come on, fish! Bite the line!" Not if they want to catch much of anything, that is.

It's the same in the Kingdom. If you want to catch a fish, you have to get out there and throw in a line. You have to go where the fish are before you can lower your net. You may have a line, but if you are not casting that line, it will do you no good. You may have a net, but if you are not throwing it into the water, it will profit you nothing. There are too many fish out there starving, dying, being carried out by the waves to eternal destruction. Fisherman, you had better get out there and catch those fish before the enemy destroys them!

Seldom will a sinner open his heart and repent on his own. They need a fisherman to guide them, to catch them and bring them into the knowledge of the truth. Be the one who casts the line, who throws the net. *"Follow Me, and I will make you fishers of men."*

And Jesus came and spake unto them, saying, All power is given unto me in heaven and in earth. Go ye therefore, and teach all nations, baptizing them in the name of the Father, and of the Son, and of the Holy Ghost: Teaching them to observe all things whatsoever I have commanded you: and, lo, I am with you alway, even unto the end of the world. Amen.   Matthew 28:18-20

There is no power and no authority higher than our Lord. He is in control of everything. And it is He who will go with us as we spread His Word.

You needn't go across the sea; there are people who need to be evangelized in your own household, in your place of employment, in the community where you live. You don't need to go far. Begin in your Jerusalem, your immediate area. Then move to your Judea, and from there to your Samaria. From Samaria, you can go to the uttermost part of the earth as the Lord grants you the opportunity. But you'll never be effective at the ends of the earth if you have not proven yourself in Jerusalem, in Judea, and in Samaria. You cannot go overseas if you are not effective in your own homeland. But don't keep debating about where to go. Just go!

The third reason we should bring souls to Christ is that Jesus is the only Savior. There is no other. Salvation is not found in a church, a denomination, or a religion. It is not found in doing good or in attempting to be good. None of these things will guarantee entrance to the Kingdom of Heaven. The only way to the Father is through Jesus Christ, the Son. He is the only Savior, the only Redeemer, the only Hope.

> *Neither is there salvation in any other: for there is none other name under heaven given among men, whereby we must be saved.* Acts 4:12

What did the angel say to Joseph?

> *And she shall bring forth a son, and thou shalt call his name Jesus: for he shall save his people from their sins.* Matthew 1:21

Jesus is the Savior, the Master, the Lord. The Gospel of Jesus Christ is the only power of God unto salvation, and it is our responsibility to bring Jesus to those who need to be introduced to Him.

> *Jesus saith unto him, I am the way, the truth, and the life: no man cometh unto the Father, but by me.* John 14:8

Christ is the only way to God. He is the only and ultimate life-giving Truth. He is the only life, and He has it to give in abundance. There is only one way into the Kingdom of Heaven, there is only one way into the heart of God, and that is through His Son.

There are many religious people, many moral people, many decent people. Sometimes the sinner is more moral than the Christians inside the churches. But without Jesus Christ, these people are still sinners, and they are still going to Hell. The only way to go to Heaven, the only way to receive salvation, the only way to partake of eternal life is to come to Jesus Christ.

> *Then said Jesus unto them again, Verily, verily, I say unto you, I am the door of the sheep. All that ever came before me are thieves and robbers: but the sheep did not hear them. I am the door: by me if any man enter in, he shall be saved, and shall go in and out, and find pasture. The thief cometh not, but for to steal, and to kill, and to destroy: I am come that they might have life, and that they might have it more abundantly.* John 10:7-10

This is why we need to proclaim the Gospel. This is why we need to reach out. There is only one way, and it is through Jesus Christ. He is the Door. No one can enter into the green pastures, finding the provision of God and experiencing His abundant life, unless they go in through Him. His name is the only one by which we can be saved, and that name dwells in you. It is up to you to bring it to others.

The fourth reason we should bring souls to Christ is that it is not only our duty and our responsibility; it is also our privilege, our honor, our blessing, and our joy. Every time I pray with someone to receive the Lord Jesus, I am flooded with joy. It is as though I were being saved all over again! What a privilege to be used of God in this way!

How wonderful it is to be called laborers together with Christ! What a blessing and honor to be working together with Him!

You are not working *for* God; you are working *with* Him. The greatest enterprise in the world is the salvation of souls. No wonder Jesus said to His father and mother, after they had searched for Him and found Him in the Temple:

How is it that ye sought me? wist ye not that I must be about my Father's business?   Luke 2:49

"Didn't you know I must be doing My Father's business?" He asked. And what is that business? It is the business of the salvation of souls, and beloved, this is a family enterprise. His business is your business. It is our business as the Church. It is a privilege to be taking care of God's business.

What does it mean to be laborers together with God? It means that He has confidence in us. It means that He trusts us and believes in us. It means that He knows He can work with us and through us. God has entrusted us with that which is most precious here on earth — the message of the Gospel and the salvation of men. What an honor and a privilege!

Again, every time I lead somebody into new life in Christ, I feel like I'm entering into salvation all over again. I remember the excitement and the joy of being born again. If you have lost the joy of your salvation, find someone with whom to share Christ, and experience the joy of being reconciled to God in your own heart by seeing others being born into the Kingdom.

And they that be wise shall shine as the brightness of the firmament; and they that turn many to righteousness as the stars for ever and ever.   Daniel 12:3

When we win souls for Christ, we become like shining lights for Him. When you present the Gospel, when you lead sinners to Christ, you are as a shining light for the Kingdom. Be a light for Jesus.

What else does the Word say about winning souls?

> *The fruit of the righteous is a tree of life; and he that winneth*
> *souls is wise.*   Proverbs 11:30

Do you want to be wise in the Kingdom of God? Do you want to be wise in the eyes of the Lord? Then start winning souls. Begin to bring people into the Kingdom of God. You will grow in wisdom.

> *The Spirit of the LORD God is upon me; because the LORD hath*
> *anointed me to preach good tidings unto the meek; he hath sent me*
> *to bind up the brokenhearted, to proclaim liberty to the captives,*
> *and the opening of the prison to them that are bound; to proclaim*
> *the acceptable year of the LORD, and the day of vengeance of our*
> *God; to comfort all that mourn ... .*   Isaiah 61:1-2

It is a blessing to be anointed by the Spirit of God. It is an honor and a privilege to be touched by the presence of God. It is our joy to be equipped by God. Isaiah the prophet saw all of these things, and he said, *"The Spirit of the Lord God is upon me; because He hath anointed me."* Why? Why has God anointed us?

Some people seem to think that we are anointed so that we can feel more spiritual or so that we can be seen as more holy than others. But that is not why we are anointed by God. Why, then, does God anoint His people? To feel good? To be excited? To dance? To laugh? No! If we look at the Word through Isaiah, we see that we are anointed to *"proclaim,"* to preach the Good News, both through our words and through our actions.

The Bible is full of accounts of people whose lives were touched by soul-winners. For instance, Elisha the prophet was a great man of God. He is the father of the double portion anointing. Many miracles were accomplished by God through him during his lifetime and even after his death. His anointed bones resurrected a dead man. But there would have been no great ministry of Elisha had it not been for Elijah who mentored him and trained him for ministry. It was Elijah who spent time with Elisha, who brought him into the supernatural power of God, and led him into the experience of God. Be an Elijah, beloved, and raise up some Elishas in your lifetime.

Think of Naaman, the captain of the Syrian army (see 2 Kings 5). He was a man of authority, influence, honor, and dignity. He had only to speak a word, and his army obeyed. But even in the midst of this great personal glory and honor, there was one problem: Naaman was a leper. He could not freely associate with other people. But we know that Naaman was cleansed of his leprosy. Why? How? Because of the testimony of his wife's little Hebrew maid. If she had kept her experience and knowledge of the things of the Lord to herself, if she had allowed fear to overtake her, if she had not spoken concerning the prophet of Israel, Naaman would not have been healed. He was healed and delivered from leprosy because of the witness and the testimony, the anointing and wisdom of that one *"little maid."*

You might be a little maid in the eyes of the world, but if you belong to the Lord, there is gold inside of you, gold that the world longs for. There are a lot of lepers around today—men and women, educated and uneducated, rich and poor—covered with sores from top to bottom. We call these sores sin. Unless we become like that little maid, they will remain in their leprosy until they die. There will be no remedy. They will be bound for Hell.

Mark chapter 2 gives the beautiful account of a man who was sick with palsy. We would say he was paralyzed. That man could have remained in that state through his whole life, except that he had one thing that many need. He had four faithful, faith-filled friends. These were caring, daring, loving men who went out of their way to carry this man to Christ, even to the extent of climbing onto the roof and making a hole to lower him down in front of Jesus. His friends were burdened for him. They were faithful to that burden and acted upon it with wonderful results.

What about Peter? He was a wonderful man of God, but his name would have remained Simon, and he would not have been a great apostle if there were no Andrew who sought him. Andrew met the Lord, and then he got a burden and a compassion for his brother. Andrew went out of his way to find Peter and bring him to the Lord. We admire Peter, but often we forget about Andrew. Peter's success could only have come about because there was an Andrew. Be an Andrew, beloved. Look for a Simon, and bring him to the Lord. God can change him into a mighty Peter.

We usually think of Paul as the great apostle, writer of a large part of the New Testament, but he was not always a believer in Christ. In fact, he persecuted Christians and was responsible for the deaths of many. Acts chapter 9 contains the dramatic account of his Damascus Road conversion. But even Paul—or Saul, as he was then known—needed someone to guide him into this new life. That person was Ananias. It was Ananias through whom God restored Saul's sight. It was he who guided Paul, nurtured him, and raised him up in the truth. It was probably Ananias who led him into the experiences of water baptism and the baptism in the Holy Spirit. Ananias spent time nurturing Saul. Be an Ananias. Find a Saul and bring him to God. He will be transformed into a mighty Paul. God can turn murderers into preachers and persecutors into builders in the Kingdom of God.

As a final example, let's look to the fourth chapter of John. Here we find the account of Christ's dealings with the woman at Jacob's well in Sychar. This woman had a bad reputation when she met the Lord at the well, and yet during their conversation, He offered her His living water. When she tasted of it, her life was transformed, completely revolutionized. She had forgotten her purpose in going to the well. She left her pot and ran to the city, proclaiming her message: "Come out! I've found the Messiah! Come out to the well! He is there!" It is amazing, but the entire city believed her words. Everyone came out, and everyone was saved. What a revival they experienced! The entire community came to the Lord Jesus Christ and was born again because of the words of this woman.

You see, these people were ready to be saved; but if the woman had not told them about Jesus, they would not have known that the Holy One was right there at the well. They would not have come to the knowledge of salvation. They would not have experienced the love of God.

It is our responsibility to follow the example of these men and women. It is our task to reach out to the lost.

Son of man, I have made thee a watchman unto the house of Israel: therefore hear the word at my mouth, and give them warning from me. When I say unto the wicked, Thou shalt surely die; and thou givest him not warning, nor speakest to warn the wicked from his wicked way, to save his life; the same wicked man shall die in his iniquity; but his blood will I require at thine hand. Yet if thou warn the wicked, and he turn not from his wickedness, nor from his wicked way, he shall die in his iniquity; but thou hast delivered thy soul. Again, When a righteous man doth turn from his righteousness, and commit iniquity, and I lay a stumbling-block before him, he shall die: because thou hast not given him warning, he shall die in his sin, and his righteousness which he hath done shall not be remembered; but his blood will I require at thine hand. Nevertheless if thou warn the righteous man, that the righteous sin not, and he doth not sin, he shall surely live, because he is warned; also thou hast delivered thy soul.

Ezekiel 3:17-21

We are the assigned watchmen. You are God's appointed watchman in your city to warn the people of the coming danger and judgment. What are you doing to increase the Kingdom? Win the lost! Be a light at your job, a witness in your community. Your family needs the Lord. Your friends need the Lord. Your neighbors need the Lord. Do not be afraid to speak to them. Focus on what you have to share with others—the greatest treasure in the earth, the life of Jesus Christ. You have experienced that life. You know the reality of it. You have felt it, tasted it, handled it, and seen it.

May the Father give us His burden for the lost, and may we live our lives in such a way that others will see Jesus in us. Allow the Lord to do a work of compassion in your heart for those who are lost, dying without Christ. There is still time, and there is still opportunity for us to do the work. It is an awesome responsibility to which we are called.

As you pray concerning this burden, think about three questions. How many souls have you brought into the Kingdom of God since you were born again? When was the last time you shared Jesus Christ with others? And when was the last time you felt the burden for lost souls?

CHAPTER 3

THE VISION FOR SOULS BECOMES OUR MISSION

Pray ye therefore the Lord of the harvest, that he will send forth labourers into his harvest. Matthew 9:38

What do you see when you look into a mirror? Do you see imperfections? When you think of your life, do you think of the failures you have experienced? Do you look at your shortcomings or do you look at your strengths?

The devil would like you to see only the failures, the imperfections, the shortcomings. He loves it when you focus on them. Why? Because then you will be feeling worthless, unusable, but that is not what God wants you to see.

When God looks at you, He says, "Beneath that clay that you see in the mirror, beneath the imperfections, there is gold. There is gold inside you that needs to be mined from deep within. That is the work of My Holy Spirit in your life. He is digging deeper and deeper, bringing out the beauty of that gold for all the world to see. And when the light of My Spirit shines in you and is reflected by that gold, you will really shine for Me!"

You may already be in labor, awaiting the birthing of the glory of the Lord in your life. You may even feel that it is almost overdue. But at the right time, the Lord will cause a birthing by His Spirit. Then will you go forth in the power and the anointing of the Holy Spirit.

Ray Llarena

As the chisel and the hammer are used in the hand of the sculptor, chipping away at everything that does not match the artist's vision, so are the dealings of God in your life. He may use your spouse, your boss, your pastor, your children, or the circumstances that surround you. These are all His tools in shaping you. It isn't always fun, and it doesn't always feel wonderful, but the Sculptor of your life must continue to work, chiseling and hammering, if He is to perfect His vision in you.

And we know that all things work together for good to them that love God, to them who are the called according to his purpose.
                                                                Romans 8:28

Are there difficulties, trials, or temptations in your life? Is there suffering and hardship? Trust in the Lord, beloved. He is the Sculptor, the master Artist. He is chiseling out every carnality, every fleshly part of you. He will continue to work until the image is completely visible to all who will look upon your life, for we are, as Paul wrote:

... confident of this very thing, that he which hath begun a good work in you will perform it until the day of Jesus Christ.
                                                                Philippians 1:6

What is this image that God is perfecting in your life? It is none other than the image of Christ Himself.

For whom he did foreknow, he also did predestinate to be conformed to the image of his Son, that he might be the firstborn among many brethren.   Romans 8:29

But we all, with open face beholding as in a glass the glory of the Lord, are changed into the same image from glory to glory, even as by the Spirit of the Lord.　　　　2 Corinthians 3:18

There is a move of God abroad in the earth. Revival is taking place. People are being healed, set free, and delivered from bondage to sin. God is moving mightily by His Spirit, and many are turning to Him. This is a glorious time to be part of the Church!

Yet, with all of the wonderful things that are going on throughout the land, we need to be careful. God is moving in a mighty way, but it would be easy to become distracted by the things that are happening in the Church. We need to be mindful of our direction. We need to be mindful of our purpose. We need to be mindful of our vision, our mission.

You cannot have a mission without a vision. When you have a vision, you have a mission. Ours is not "Mission Impossible." Our mission is possible because we can do all things through Christ who strengthens us (see Philippians 4:13).

This is a time for seeking the Lord. Allow Him to work in your heart and in your life. Look for Him to begin to change you, to shape you more closely into His image. He will perfect your calling in Him. He will transform you, bringing you more in tune with His will. Allow Him to have His way in you. Usually what hinders the moving of the Spirit is not the Lord, and it isn't even the sinners. Usually it is a lack of fervency on the part of believers, a lack of desire to be transformed into the image of Christ.

Many among the Body of Christ are experiencing revival. There is a brokenness before the Lord, and His presence is being manifested as God works in hearts and lives. When I was before the Lord recently, worshiping and asking the Lord to search my heart, praying for the ministry of the local church, crying—the tears flowing freely—for a visitation from God, and asking God to have mercy upon us, the Lord gave me a vision. It lasted only a brief time, but it was clear. I saw a ball of fire. It grew and grew until it was quite large. It had a tail like a comet. It was very bright. And then the Spirit of God began to speak to my heart. He said, "I'm going to send the fire of the Holy Ghost into the midst of the Church, and there shall be a mighty Holy Ghost revival."

And He has been faithful to that vision. The glory of the Lord has been present in our meetings, our times of corporate worship have been beautiful before the Lord, and people are being slain in the Spirit, healed, and delivered. God is working in a real way, He is moving among us, and He is waiting to move among all His people.

Beloved, we must prepare ourselves for the things that are about to take place. Those who will not run with the vision will be left behind. Those who are willing to run with it will find their destiny in God. So run with the vision of God! Walk in it daily. Live in His vision. Fulfill the commission that He has given to you and to me.

We have seen that the commission, the vision of God for us, is to win souls. We have seen that this is the command of the Lord. It is also that which is closest to the heart of God. Christ came to seek and to save that which was lost. If He had not come to fulfill God's mission, where would we be today? If Christ had not come, where would men find salvation?

Your life in Christ is the result of the vision of God. You are part of the fulfillment of the mission of Christ. But Jesus left us a task that we must continue. He said, *"Occupy until I come"* (Luke 19:13).

We are to be active until He comes. We are to take control, to have dominion, until He comes. We are to be living for Him, involved in the work that He has given us to do. We cannot be lazy. That is not an option. We cannot simply pass our responsibility off to someone else. We must lay hold of it if we are to pursue the vision.

Have you ever watched the Olympics? The Kingdom of God is like the Olympic torch. Someone runs with the torch, but he gets tired, so he passes it off to someone else, saying, "Keep running!" That person grows weary and passes it on, saying, "Keep running!" When the next person is worn out, he passes on the torch. The important thing is to pass the torch, that the runners may keep running with it. Jesus says to us today, "I am passing to you the torch. I am passing to you the message. I am entrusting to you the keys of the Kingdom. I am passing to you the authority to open the prison doors and to release the captives, to shine forth My light, to give sight to the blind. I am giving you the authority, the dominion, and the power so you can bring people into the Kingdom. Occupy till I come!"

The torch is in your hand. Run with it! Pass it on to someone else. You have been born into the Kingdom. Now bring others in. We were not saved simply so that we could one day go to Heaven; we were brought to God that we might establish His Kingdom on earth. That is God's desire. It is the prayer Christ taught His disciples to pray.

Thy kingdom come. Thy will be done in earth, as it is in heaven. Matthew 6:10

How are we to expand God's Kingdom and bring it to the earth? By our obedience to the things He has given us to do. So how do we go about accomplishing this first mission of winning souls? Let's look to the Bible. Christ Jesus said:

Ye are the light of the world. A city that is set on an hill cannot be hid. Neither do men light a candle, and put it under a bushel, but on a candlestick; and it giveth light unto all that are in the house. Let your light so shine before men, that they may see your good works, and glorify your Father which is in heaven.

Matthew 5:14-16

Go ye therefore, and teach all nations, baptizing them in the name of the Father, and of the Son, and of the Holy Ghost: Teaching them to observe all things whatsoever I have commanded you: and, lo, I am with you alway, even unto the end of the world. Amen.

Matthew 28:19-20

We are to demonstrate the power of God when we preach the Word. We are to release the anointing of the Lord God when we preach the Gospel so that the sick are delivered and the oppressed set free. Those on whom we lay our hands will receive the power of God, and an anointing will come upon us that will demonstrate the power of God to all who believe.

Soul-winning has two parts. The first is the salvation of the lost. We must win the lost, bringing them into the Kingdom and helping them to know Jesus Christ. They need to begin to understand the purpose of the plan of God for their lives. Our mission is to point the way to the cross. We are to let them know and understand the reality of Jesus Christ, showing them how to open their hearts to the Lord. As we present the message of the Gospel, we are, in reality, showing them the way of escape and deliverance—Jesus Christ, the Savior, the Lord, the risen Master who is coming again.

God's Word is sure. He truly is the Way, the Truth, and the Life, and no man can come to the Father except through Him (see John 14:6). There really is only one name given under Heaven by which we might be saved, and that name is Jesus Christ (see Acts 4:12). His name was to be Jesus, for He would save His people from their sins (see Matthew 1:21). The Gospel of Jesus Christ is still the power of God unto salvation to everyone who believes (see Romans 1:16). Our responsibility is to present the Good News. We are to proclaim the Gospel, to testify of Jesus Christ, and to introduce the world to the Savior.

The second part of soul-winning is the discipling of the new believers. Our job is not finished once sinners are won to Christ. We still need to complete our task. New believers need to be discipled, educated, trained, nurtured, and taught if they are to grow and to be effective and mature in Christ. Discipleship includes training, guiding, teaching, strengthening, encouraging, edifying, and mentoring. It includes all of the things that will enable a new believer to live a vital life in Christ and to become like Him. Discipleship also trains new Christians so that they may go forth and do the work of the ministry. What should they do? They should go out and win the lost.

Have you ever wanted to witness but were afraid to do so because you felt you did not know how to go about it? Well, training is important. But practice is even more important. And it does not have to be so difficult. If you are not enjoying your relationship with Jesus Christ, you will not share it with others. If you are enjoying that relationship, you will not be able to keep it to yourself!

You will talk about it with those you care about and with those you meet. That is what witnessing is all about. That's evangelizing, and it is also discipleship. You are encouraging others to follow you in your walk with Jesus Christ.

Jesus said, *"Follow Me, and I will make you fishers of men"* (Matthew 4:19). He was with His disciples for three and a half years, teaching them how to fish. That was discipleship. You who are saved, you who have been born into the Kingdom of God, you need discipleship. You need training. That is how you learn to fulfill your mission to win souls for the glory of God.

> *But ye shall receive power, after that the Holy Ghost is come upon you: and ye shall be witnesses unto me both in Jerusalem, and in all Judaea, and in Samaria, and unto the uttermost part of the earth.*   Acts 1:8

Do you have the power of God? Have you been born into the Kingdom, and has the Holy Ghost *"come upon"* you? Then live in that power. You have access to it. In fact, you were born into it when you received the Lord Jesus.

> *But as many as received him, to them gave he power to become the sons of God, even to them that believe on his name: which were born, not of blood, nor of the will of the flesh, nor of the will of man, but of God.*   John 1:12-13

When you were born into this physical world, there were no choices for you. You did not choose when or where you were to be born. You did not choose your parents or family. You did not choose what you would look like. This is similar to your birth into the family of God. It did not happen by the will of man or of the flesh. You were born into the Kingdom by the will of God, and you were born with power in the spiritual realm.

> *Grace be to you, and peace, from God our Father, and from the Lord Jesus Christ. Blessed be the God and Father of our Lord Jesus Christ, who hath blessed us with all spiritual blessings in heavenly places in Christ.* Ephesians 1:2-3

God has given you *"all spiritual blessings"* in Christ. Certainly that includes the power and the ability to witness for Him.

Whether you like it or not, you are a witness for Christ. People will look into your life to see whether the faith you profess makes any real difference. They will look at your words, your actions, and your attitudes. What does your witness speak to others concerning the life in Christ that you profess?

When we look at Acts 1:8, we see that the disciples were instructed to witness in various realms: Jerusalem, Judea, Samaria, and the uttermost part of the earth. One way of viewing this is in terms of geographical location, or witnessing to your immediate vicinity and then moving out to increasingly larger areas. Another way to look at this is in terms of your spheres of influence. This would include your home, your workplace, your community, and then larger spheres as the Lord directs.

As a believer, you should not have to pray, "Lord, send someone to witness to my family." You are already there for them. The Lord will honor your witness and ministry to your loved ones. As they see the changes the Lord brings to your life, they will become hungry for the same spiritual life and food.

> *And brought them out, and said, Sirs, what must I do to be saved? And they* [Paul and Silas] *said, Believe on the Lord Jesus Christ, and thou shalt be saved, and thy house.* Acts 16:30-31

Your household will be saved as each member beholds your salvation. As each person sees you working out your salvation and sees the transformation that is taking place in your life, then they, too, will be drawn to the Lord. When you were saved and delivered, you became a part of the family of God. You have entered into a relationship with Him. You have also become a priest unto God:

> *But ye are a chosen generation, a royal priesthood, an holy nation, a peculiar people; that ye should show forth the praises of him who hath called you out of darkness into his marvellous light.*
> 1 Peter 2:9

According to Peter, you have become a member of the royal priesthood for a reason: that you might show forth the praises of God. Ultimately, it doesn't really matter who you are. You may be young or old, rich or poor, educated or not, but the moment you were saved, you became the priest to your own family.

Please don't misunderstand me. This is not a position of authority for lording it over others; it is a place of spiritual authority whereby you can proclaim in the spiritual realms: "This family belongs to the Lord!" This is a place of spiritual service, wherein you lovingly show forth the life and love of the Lord to your loved ones.

There was something special about the clothing the Old Testament priests wore. This is explained in the book of Exodus:

> *And Aaron shall bear the names of the children of Israel in the breastplate of judgment upon his heart, when he goeth in unto the holy place, for a memorial before the Lord continually.*
>
> Exodus 28:29

Aaron and the other Levitical high priests carried the names of the twelve tribes of Israel about with them on their breastplate, over their hearts. In the same way, you are to carry the names of your family about with you in your heart, praying, interceding, believing, and standing in the gap for them.

You are a priest, one who ministers before the Lord and, as such, you need to carry the names of your own tribe, or family, before Him. Sometimes people say, "Why is my whole family not saved yet? I'm believing in God." They may be believing in God, but are they living for Him? Believing in God doesn't mean that you're living for Him. Are you living for God? Are you changed? Are you being transformed daily by the renewing of your mind? If you are allowing God to change you, if you are praying, and if you are reading the Word, then you don't need to preach. Sometimes you don't need to say a word. Your life will do the preaching as you let the light shine. Your changed heart will speak clearly of the life that is manifesting itself deep within you. Your husband or your wife, your children, your parents, your brother or your sister must see the change, the transformation that has taken place in your life. The best way to witness is to allow others to see the new life that you profess.

If you confess that you have been born again, and yet there is no change in your life, you are witnessing another way. You are saying that God has no relevance to your life. You are saying that He has no power to transform souls. You are saying that God cannot do a work for you, and He will also not do it for anyone else.

I am not saying that you must be perfect, but you should be changed. You should be in the process of being perfected, of maturing in God. Change may be gradual, but it should be occurring, one change at a time. Even Paul did not claim to have been transformed entirely overnight, although there was a dramatic immediate change in his life.

> *But we all, with open face beholding as in a glass the glory of the Lord, are changed into the same image from glory to glory, even as by the Spirit of the Lord.* 2 Corinthians 3:18

We, too, are changing step by step and from glory to glory. But we *are* being changed. God is changing us. You don't need to blow a trumpet and proclaim that you are a Christian. People will know you are a Christian if you are living for God. You don't need to worry about how to approach others about Christ. All you need to do is to live in Christ, and they will see a life that has been transformed by Him.

> *Ye are my witnesses, saith the LORD, and my servant whom I have chosen: that ye may know and believe me, and understand that I am he: before me there was no God formed, neither shall there be after me.* Isaiah 43:10

We are His witnesses, the witnesses of Christ. Do you believe God has called you to be His witness? Then do it! If you don't, you are being disobedient to God. We are not just witnesses; we are also servants. In other words, we are sent out to accomplish the purpose of the One who has sent us. Let us be obedient servants.

Witnessing is serving God. It is one of the responsibilities of a servant—to witness concerning his master, to talk about the master, to proclaim the master's greatness.

Isaiah said that God has chosen us to be His witnesses. What a wonderful truth! He could have sent angels. He could have written on the walls, He could have shown forth His message in the clouds, or He could have proclaimed His tidings in the thunder, but He did not.

Instead, God has chosen you. In spite of your imperfections, in spite of your shortcomings, He has chosen you and called you to be a servant who will witness for Him. The only way that your family, your friends, your neighbors, and those you meet will know God and put their faith in Christ is if you become a witness and a servant of God. This is your responsibility, and you have been chosen for this task, this privilege, this joy. *"That ye may know and believe me, and understand that I am he."*

There is no god besides our God. There is no salvation other than through Jesus Christ. But the only way others will know about the Way, the Truth, and the Life is if you proclaim Him. He is the Love, the Joy, the Strength. There is none other! He is the Wonderful Counselor, the Mighty God, and the Prince of Peace. He is the Alpha and Omega, the Beginning and the End, the Rose of Sharon, the Lily of the Valley, the Bright and Morning Star. He is everything! Beside Him there is no other.

Nothing can compare to the excellency of God's greatness, majesty, glory, and power. It should excite you to witness for Him. It should excite you to bring people into His Kingdom. It should excite you to invite people to your local church.

What does a witness do? He witnesses. In other words, he testifies. He speaks forth on behalf of others. There are two kinds of witness: a true witness and a false witness. What kind of a witness are you? It's not how well we preach that matters; it's how well we live our lives.

Witness is a judicial term. A case is being presented in court, and the judge says to a lawyer, "Bring in your witness." When the person comes to testify, he is sworn in, with his hand placed on a Bible. "Do you swear to tell the truth, the whole truth, and nothing but the truth, so help you God?" It is a familiar scene.

Well, beloved, you are that witness. You are being called and summoned to take the stand. And you had better tell the truth, so help you God. Speak the truth! Proclaim it! Tell others of the riches of the Kingdom of God. You are called to take the stand. And the life of the accused depends on you!

Yes, the very life of the one who is brought into court depends on you. The life of the accused, the sinners around you, depends on you, on your testimony, on your witness. Your testimony, your life, can either set him free or sentence him to prison or death. The life of your husband or wife, the lives of your children, the lives of your parents, depend on your witness. The lives of the people with whom you work depend on your witness. Are you willing to tell them the truth? Are you willing to speak it forth? Or will your fears close your mouth?

In a courtroom, the testimony of the witness cannot be based on hearsay. If a witness's testimony is to be effective, he must have been present and he must have seen and heard that of which he testifies. He must know how it happened, why it happened, where it happened, and the outcome after it happened. And it is the same with us. We can testify only concerning that which we know to be true. We can witness only of fact, not of fantasy.

Many believers seem to be living in a fantasy world when it comes to their spiritual lives. They know what they want to believe, what they have heard and hope is true, but we cannot show forth that which is not real in our lives. We need reality in our spiritual lives, and that is all we can witness to. That is what will bring life.

That which was from the beginning, which we have heard, which we have seen with our eyes, which we have looked upon, and our hands have handled, of the Word of life; (for the life was manifested, and we have seen it, and bear witness, and show unto you that eternal life, which was with the Father, and was manifested unto us;) that which we have seen and heard declare we unto you, that ye also may have fellowship with us: and truly our fellowship is with the Father, and with his Son Jesus Christ. 1 John 1:1-3

What will save souls is not the doctrines of Christ, nor is it the teachings of Christ. It is also not the principles of Christ nor the guidelines of Christ. It is the Person of Jesus Christ. Many people are mastering the doctrines, but they are not mastering the Person. Many are mastering the way, but they are not mastering He who is the Way. Many are mastering the teaching without mastering the Teacher. Even if you don't know much about the Gospel, if you know the Person of Jesus Christ, if you have experienced His power to transform your life, then you are a witness and an effective one.

Get acquainted with Christ. Know Him; surrender to Him. Allow Jesus Christ to take dominion and control over your life. Please understand this: you can know the Gospel and still go to Hell. But if you know the Lord Jesus Christ, if He is living in you, then you will go to Heaven, even if John 3:16 is the only Bible verse you know.

The early Church lived a life that testified of Christ. What did people say of them?

> *And when they found them not, they drew Jason and certain brethren unto the rulers of the city, crying, These that have turned the world upside down are come hither also; whom Jason hath received: and these all do contrary to the decrees of Caesar, saying that there is another king, one Jesus.* Acts 17:6-7

"These people have turned the world upside down! They are declaring that Jesus is their King!" They had a witness. People could see that they were believers who knew Jesus.

Beloved, the greatest tragedy that we can find in the Gospel, the greatest cry of the people of the world, is found in Psalm 142:

> *I looked on my right hand, and beheld, but there was no man that would know me: refuge failed me; no man cared for my soul.*
> Psalm 142:4

"No man cared for my soul!" I pray that you will begin to care for the lost, for the sinners, and that you will begin to respond to them in love and compassion, touching them with the hand of Jesus and leading them to the foot of the cross of Calvary.

This is important, beloved. Souls are going to Hell because the Church is not doing its job. Individual believers are not doing their job. Our job, our mission, is not to meet together with other believers to worship and praise God, as enjoyable as that is. It is not to pray together, fellowship together, and minister to one another. We are not to be focused on one another! Our mission is to go forth to the harvest. When we meet together, we are to rejoice over the harvest and give glory to God for it.

When we speak the truth, regardless of who gets hurt or offended, we are true witnesses. When we don't compromise the truth, regardless of what we might gain or lose, we are good witnesses. When we overcome temptation, we are good witnesses. When we rejoice and praise God in the midst of difficult situations, we are good witnesses. When we live for Christ in spite of persecution, we are good witnesses. When we say, "No, I don't do that. I don't partake of those things because I'm a child of God"—even if we lose friends—we are good witnesses.

Compromise is contrary to witnessing. Can you be a faithful witness? Yes, you can. Ask the Lord to give you an opportunity to share Christ. Ask Him to lay someone on your heart, someone you can pray for and witness to, and He will do it.

CHAPTER 4

LEARNING TO MINISTER TO OTHERS

Wherefore seeing we also are compassed about with so great a cloud of witnesses, let us lay aside every weight, and the sin which doth so easily beset us, and let us run with patience the race that is set before us.   Hebrews 12:1

The first aspect of God's vision for us is soul-winning, and the second is that which will help us to win souls. If we embrace this part of God's vision for the Church, our Christian lives will be revitalized, and our lights will blaze forth as our lives are transformed and as we gain in the ability to minister to others' needs. This aspect is prayer.

There is power in prayer! Have you seen that prayer works in your life? Have you found out yet that nothing is impossible when you pray? Do you know that nothing is too difficult when you know how to pray?

If you have needs or problems in your life, if you have difficulties with finances or with health, if you have children who are running away from God or friends or loved ones who are not yet saved, then you have reason to pray. You have reason to fervently seek God.

Prayer is an awesome thing. It is a privilege that God has given to us. When you begin to pray, you are giving yourself into the hands of God. When you begin to pray, you are saying, "There is hope. There is a remedy. There is an answer for me in God."

God wants His Church to be a praying Church, and He expects His people to be a praying people. It is His desire that we pray, and this should be our desire as well. If it is not, then we can ask Him and God will give us grace to grow in this area.

Prayer is so very important. Unless we pray, we will never see the hand of God moving. Unless we pray, we will never see miracles taking place. Unless we pray, we will never see the real changes that need to take place in our lives. We need to pray!

Prayer is an important opportunity, a privilege that God has given to His people. Prayer is the point at which we may access God's power, and it is the key that unlocks the doors of Heaven. Prayer allows us to enter into the supernatural realm so that we can experience God. That is when God will begin to transform our lives. Prayer is the one activity that will bring us to the fullness of God's glory.

Prayer is crucial. No wonder Jesus' life was one of prayer. If you read the gospels and look at the description of Christ's life, you will soon notice that He was always praying. He was praying in the morning, praying in the afternoon, praying in the evening, and even throughout the night.

We see this among the believers in the accounts of the early Church as well. It was a Church whose people prayed, and, as a result, it was a time of great power and miracles. No wonder the very shadow of the disciples brought healing and deliverance! No wonder there were so many healings, so that even the dead were raised! These were people of prayer!

Prayer is not something to debate, it is not something to read about, nor is it something to teach. There is nothing wrong with discussing and reading and learning and teaching, but prayer should not be just another good sermon topic. Prayer is to be something that we do, something that we practice. Prayer is to be something that we live, a part of who we are.

And [Jesus] *said unto them, It is written, My house shall be called the house of prayer; but ye have made it a den of thieves.*
Matthew 21:13

When you go into a church building, you are not going into the House of God, as so many think. You *are* the house or the temple of God. When you go to church, you are going to a house of prayer. Your home is also to be a house of prayer. When your home, your church, and your life become houses of prayer, you will begin to experience the power of God.

I believe God is ready to pour forth a mighty blessing upon His Church. It is already being poured out in some places. But it can only happen when we begin to seriously pray and seek Him.

We know that the Bible is the written Word of God. It is God's love letter to us who have fallen in love with Him. The Bible reveals who God is. It records what God has done, and it contains the accounts of many men and women who have gone before us. But the Bible is also something else. It is a record book of prayers prayed and prayers answered. It is the story of ordinary men and women—people who faced problems, temptations, sufferings, trials, frailties, and sicknesses, but these men and women discovered the power of prayer and gave themselves to it. The Bible is the account of how they discovered the supernatural release of God's power that transformed their lives. The Bible is the record of the lives of ordinary men and women who touched the throne of God and found the power of the Lord that brought deliverance to the oppressed and salvation and healing to people in need.

Every time I read the Bible, I see men and women like you and me. I see people who faced temptation, people who knew limitations. They had their shortcomings. They were encompassed about with many difficulties. But there is one thing I have discovered: the men and women who walk the pages of the Book discovered the power of prayer. They tasted and experienced the possibilities of prayer, and they found out what God could do and would do if men and women would only begin to pray.

It is easy to grow discouraged, feeling overwhelmed by the necessities of everyday life. This seems to be a normal mindset for our society today. There is always so much to do, so many places to go, and so many things that need to be dealt with. Too often, we in the Church have bought into this sentiment, and it is easy to feel hopeless and despairing. But, beloved, this need not be! There is a way of escape for us—the door of prayer. We can find rest, comfort, and consolation, deliverance, healing, salvation, provision, and supply in our God.

God has an inexhaustible provision and supply for His people. He is El Shaddai, the God who is more than enough. He is Jehovah-Jireh, the God who supplies. He is Jehovah-Shammah, the God who is ever-present.

When you are discouraged, look to the accounts of prayers that are written in the Bible, the stories of men and women who were found to be in the valley of need. For instance, envision Luke's account of the mother who was brokenhearted because her only son had died (see Luke 7:12-17). This woman was a widow, and now she had lost her son as well. Imagine the grief in that woman's heart! When we first see her, she is part of a funeral procession, going to bury her dear son. But that widow was one of God's own. God heard the prayer of her heart, and He sent Jesus to her, just as He will for you and me. God sent His Son to bring life to this woman's son.

Are your loved ones dead in trespasses and sin? Then know that when you pray earnestly, believing that the Lord will intervene, the resurrection power of God can flow into their lives. Then they will walk out of the grave of sin into freedom and liberty. They will experience the forgiveness of sin, embrace the gift of eternal life, and find their names written in the Lamb's Book of Life. Then you will see them rejoicing in the presence of God. But these things will only begin to happen when we seriously seek God with all our hearts in prayer.

It is time for us to stop playing games with God and to become serious in our relationship with Him. Let us seek God as never before. Let us examine our hearts, making sure that we are sensitive in our spirits to hear the voice of God. Spend time in prayer. Prayer will bring you out from your selfishness, your carnality, your pride, your self-righteousness, and your criticism. Prayer—prayer that is pure, unselfish, and righteous—will bring you out from everything that is sinful or fleshly in your life. This kind of prayer will purify you, sanctify you, and make you holy. It will transform you. You cannot touch the heart of the Lord, spending time in quietness before Him listening to the whisper of His Spirit, without being changed.

Many people do not pray because they know that when they begin to pray seriously, God will deal with their hearts. There are those who are afraid to pray because they are afraid of being confronted by things that need to be changed in their lives. Change is not easy, especially if there are things that need to be uprooted from your heart. But change is necessary.

The account of Abraham is a clear example of the power of prayer. In Genesis chapter 18 we find Abraham, a man of God, conversing with the angel of the Lord. This angel has told him that God is going to send judgment upon Sodom and Gomorrah. God's wrath has reached its limit, and His grace has come to an end. It is time for the people of these towns to reap what they have sown, and so judgment is coming to their cities. And what was Abraham's response?

Abraham began to intercede. His nephew lived in Sodom. Lot's wife, his sons and daughters, and his sons-in-law all lived in that land of sin. So Abraham began to plead on their behalf:

And the men turned their faces from thence, and went toward Sodom: but Abraham stood yet before the LORD. And Abraham drew near, and said, Wilt thou also destroy the righteous with the wicked? Peradventure there be fifty righteous within the city: wilt thou also destroy and not spare the place for the fifty righteous that are therein? That be far from thee to do after this manner, to slay the righteous with the wicked: and that the righteous should be as the wicked, that be far from thee: shall not the Judge of all the earth do right?

And the LORD said, If I find in Sodom fifty righteous within the city, then I will spare all the place for their sakes.

And Abraham answered and said, Behold now, I have taken upon me to speak unto the LORD, which am but dust and ashes: peradventure there shall lack five of the fifty righteous: wilt thou destroy all the city for lack of five?

And he said, If I find there forty and five, I will not destroy it.
Genesis 18:22-28

Abraham continued to intercede for his relatives, pleading with God because of his burden for them. He finally requested that the towns be spared if only ten righteous people were found within. He must have felt that surely Lot would have made at least that many converts!

In his travailing for Lot and his family, Abraham spoke to God as to a man. He pleaded, he argued, and he pleaded some more. His burden was great, because he did not want his nephew and his family to be consumed by the wrath of God.

Think about that. Abraham's heart was soft for his kindred. He was a God-fearing man, yet he was not afraid to intercede and try to bargain with God in this way. What about you? You probably have family, friends, or acquaintances who are about to be consumed by the anger and wrath of God. Wake up, beloved! We need to stand in the gap. We need to plead, to intercede, to cry out to the Lord for our families, for our spouses, for our children, for our parents and our friends, for the time of judgment is coming.

God heard Abraham's prayer and sent an angel to help Lot and his family escape the judgment that was coming to Sodom. And the God who heard Abraham will also hear you.

Another man who learned the power of prayer was Jacob. He was a man who lived up to his name. He was a deceiver. He had deceived his father, cheated his brother, and run away from home because his sin had found him out.

When Jacob ran, he ended up working for Laban, his mother's brother. The Lord blessed him there, giving him wives and children, and making him wealthy. However, when the Lord's blessing upon his life became obvious, his uncle no longer wanted Jacob around. After all, it was Laban's flocks that were enriching Jacob.

> *And Jacob beheld the countenance of Laban, and, behold, it was not toward him as before. And the* LORD *said unto Jacob, Return unto the land of thy fathers, and to thy kindred; and I will be with thee.* Genesis 31:2-3

God began to stir Jacob's spirit. It was time for him to go home. I believe that Rebekah had probably been longing for her son and was probably praying for his return, like so many parents who long for their children to come home. Rebekah's mother-heart was troubled for her son, and so she interceded on his behalf, pouring out her heart before God for his return, that she might see him once more.

So Jacob gathered his family and his possessions and began the journey back to his father's house. As they traveled, Jacob sent messengers before him to his brother, Esau. These were to let his bother know that he was coming and to prepare the way for him so that his brother would understand that he was coming in peace. However, the message the servants brought back was ominous:

> *And the messengers returned to Jacob, saying, We came to thy brother Esau, and also he cometh to meet thee, and four hundred men with him.* Genesis 32:6

Oh, my! Esau was so glad to see Jacob that he was bringing an army out to meet him! What could Jacob do? He decided to try to placate his brother. He sent some servants ahead of him with gifts for Esau, flocks and herds of the animals he had with him. But just in case this did not work, he divided his family and servants into two groups, so that one group could escape in case of attack. And then he did something beautiful.

> *And Jacob was left alone; and there wrestled a man with him until the breaking of the day. And when he saw that he prevailed not against him, he touched the hollow of his thigh; and the hollow of Jacob's thigh was out of joint, as he wrestled with him.*
> *And he said, Let me go, for the day breaketh.*
> *And he said, I will not let thee go, except thou bless me.*
> *And he said unto him, What is thy name?*
> *And he said, Jacob.*
> *And he said, Thy name shall be called no more Jacob, but Israel: for as a prince hast thou power with God and with men, and hast prevailed.* Genesis 32:24-28

Instead of being afraid and discouraged, Jacob went to a place where he could be alone with God. There he had a most beautiful experience. This happened even though it was a time of desperation, danger, anguish, need, and crisis in Jacob's life. He knew there was a remedy to his difficulties, and because of this knowledge, he went to the Source who could meet his needs. He went to the Lord in prayer.

Jacob wrestled with the angel of the Lord, saying, "I am determined. I am not going to quit. I'm not going to stop praying until he blesses me." Jacob named that place Peniel (see verse 30). What is the significance of this place? Peniel is the place of prayer, of communion with God. It is that sacred, holy place where you are alone with God. It is the place to which you go when you come to the end of your own strength and your own resources. There, at Peniel, you can put yourself into God's hands. Beloved, you will never discover the fullness of God until you come to the end of yourself. You need to find a Peniel in your life. We all do. Take the time to cross a river in your spiritual life. Take the time to be alone with God.

When Jacob was at Peniel, he was determined. He was not going to let go! We need that same determination in God. When we come to the Lord in prayer, we need to come with the attitude of Jacob. "I'm not going to give up until I see my wayward child serving the Lord." "I won't give up until I see my husband (or my wife) give his (her) life to the Lord." "I refuse defeat until I see my parents come to God."

Prayer is wrestling with the promises and the power of God. It is taking hold tightly of God Himself and not letting go. Jacob said, "I will not let you go unless you bless me." But God had already blessed him beyond and above what he could have asked!

The angel of the Lord asked, "What is your name?"

Jacob answered honestly, "Jacob." In other words, he was admitting, "I am a cheater, a liar, a deceiver. I have even taken advantage of my father and my brother."

But, because he had touched the power of God through prayer, the angel said, "Now you are no longer Jacob, but Israel, prince of God; for you have prevailed with God and with man."

Prayer is an awesome thing! It is powerful, majestic, and supernatural. Prayer is the one thing that can revolutionize your life. It will change your attitude, your mind, your conduct, and your character. Your behavior, your life-style, and even your destiny will be transformed by the power of prayer.

The book of James has something to say about an Old Testament man of prayer:

> *Elias was a man subject to like passions as we are, and he prayed earnestly that it might not rain: and it rained not on the earth by the space of three years and six months. And he prayed again, and the heaven gave rain, and the earth brought forth her fruit.*   James 5:17-18

Elias, or Elijah, prayed earnestly, although he was *"subject to like passions as we are."* There was really no difference between Elijah and us. He was not created as somehow more spiritual, or better able to pray. He was not formed with a greater access to God than is available to us today. In fact, we are able to come before the Lord with a greater degree of freedom, for we have the Lord Jesus Christ in our lives, and it is He who intercedes for us.

I admire Elijah. He was a great man of God. But there was no difference between him and us. Elijah was a common, ordinary man. He had passions like ours, conditions like ours, trials like ours, and sufferings like ours. God performed many miracles through Elijah, and He brought revival and spiritual cleansing to Israel through the obedience of this man. Yet Elijah was still so afraid of the threats of a woman named Jezebel that he ran for his life and hid in a cave, crying out to God to take his life. He complained, and he murmured, but he also did one more thing: Elijah prayed.

Elijah knew the power of prayer. The difference between him and us is simply this: he knew how to pray. The difference is that he did not give in to temptation. He did not give in to discouragement.

Elijah had discovered that prayer can do something beautiful in the midst of an ugly situation.

God will work on your behalf in your situation too. Instead of feeling sorry for yourself or blaming others for your problems, go to the Lord in prayer.

And he said unto me, My grace is sufficient for thee: for my strength is made perfect in weakness. Most gladly therefore will I rather glory in my infirmities, that the power of Christ may rest upon me. 2 Corinthians 12:9

In your weakness, God is your strength. In your limitation, He is your power. In your need, He is your supply. Begin to pray! Practice prayer, and ask the Lord to teach you to pray effectively. Elijah was a man who was accustomed to prayer. In his time of need, he knew where to turn, and his Lord heard and answered his prayer.

It is such a beautiful thing to know that God chooses ordinary people. He is not looking for "super-Christians," but for ordinary people who will take Him at His Word, who will step out in faith, who will look to Him in the midst of their circumstances. God is looking for those who are willing to see His power and the awesomeness of His glory. His heart is after those who will begin to cry out to Him and reach out to Him. God has promised (and His promises are true).

Call unto me, and I will answer thee, and show thee great and mighty things, which thou knowest not. Jeremiah 33:3

During the time of Elijah, the wicked Ahab was king, and the evil Jezebel was his queen. The entire nation of Israel, it seemed, was given over to idolatry and the worship of Baal. Obviously, this was not what God wanted, so He sent Elijah.

In 1 Kings chapter 18, we read of the challenge Elijah issued to the followers of Baal:

Let them therefore give us two bullocks; and let them choose one bullock for themselves, and cut it in pieces, and lay it on wood, and put no fire under: and I will dress the other bullock, and lay it on wood, and put no fire under: and call ye on the name of your gods, and I will call on the name of the LORD: and the God that answereth by fire, let him be God. And all the people answered and said, It is well spoken.   1 Kings 18:23-24*

Everyone went up to Mount Carmel, and there the prophets of Baal built their altar. They prayed. They danced. They shouted. Then, when those things did not work, they cut their bodies so that the blood flowed freely before Baal. They did these things all day, but with no answer from their god.

Elijah waited until the time was right. At the time of the evening sacrifice to the Lord, he said, "It's my turn!" He built an altar, setting up twelve rocks to represent the twelve tribes of Israel. He dug a ditch around the altar. He cut wood and laid the sacrifice upon it. Finally, he doused it all with water. And, remember, this was during a time of severe drought. He did this three times.

And it came to pass at the time of the offering of the evening sacrifice, that Elijah the prophet came near, and said, LORD God of Abraham, Isaac, and of Israel, let it be known this day that thou art God in Israel, and that I am thy servant, and that I have done all these things at thy word. Hear me, O Lord, hear me, that this people may know that thou art the Lord God, and that thou hast turned their heart back again. Then the fire of the Lord fell, and consumed the burnt sacrifice, and the wood, and the stones, and the dust, and licked up the water that was in the trench.

1 Kings 18:38-38

Elijah lifted up his voice to God, but his was not an oratorical prayer. He did not pray with excellence of speech. His prayer was not even lengthy. He prayed very simply to his God. He began, *"Lord God of Abraham, Isaac, and of Israel."* He was praying to the God of covenant, of promise, and of blessing. When we come to the Lord in prayer, we are coming before this same God. We can pray, "There is a covenant and a promise; therefore give us a blessing."

Before Elijah could say, "Amen," the fire fell. The sacrifice, the wood, the water, the altar, even the dust were all consumed. Nothing was left except the power, the presence, and the glory of God. Nothing remained except the evidence that God answers prayer.

We need to pray until every bit of ourselves is consumed by the fire of God. We need to pray until there is nothing of us left to be seen. We need to pray until all that will be seen is the glory, the presence, and the power of God that is evident in our lives. It can happen. It's now your turn. It's now your time. Build your altar. Prepare your sacrifice. Remember the covenant, think about the promise, and release the blessing.

How desperate are you for God to move in your life? How desperate are you to see the power of the Lord in your life, in the life of your church, in your community, in your nation? If you truly want the Lord, then pray.

God has promised that He will hear your voice when you pray. He will answer your cry, and He will meet your need. Elijah barely had time to finish his prayer before the fire struck. In a split second, the fire of God consumed everything—the sacrifice, the wood, the stones, the water and even the dust! Nothing was left except the glory of God.

When you begin to pray, you touch the power of God, and God moves on your behalf, everything will be consumed by the power of God. Nothing will be left behind for others to see except the evidence of the power of God, the glory of God, and the manifestation of the supernatural that has taken place. Prayer is such an awesome privilege!

Elijah spent the last part of his life training a man to take his place as prophet to Israel. That man was Elisha. Now, after Elijah had died, the king of Aram was coming up against Israel. The Lord would warn Elisha of the enemy's movements, and he would warn his king. This happened several times, enraging the king of Aram. So the king sent someone to take Elisha. His army soon arrived in Dothan, where the prophet was.

And when the servant of the man of God was risen early, and gone forth, behold, an host compassed the city both with horses and chariots. And his servant said unto him, Alas, my master! how shall we do? And he answered, Fear not: for they that be with us are more than they that be with them. And Elisha prayed, and said, Lord, I pray thee, open his eyes, that he may see. And the Lord opened the eyes of the young man; and he saw: and, behold, the mountain was full of horses and chariots of fire round about Elisha. 2 Kings 6:15-18

Do you realize that doubt will cause you to see things that frighten you? Unbelief will show you things that will kill you. But faith enables you to see things that will encourage you. It will allow you to see things that lift you up in victory. It will encourage you and energize you so that you can leap up to overcome the enemy.

Elisha said, "Lord, open his eyes, that he may see." Yes, Lord! Open our eyes ! Open the eyes of Your Church, that we may see Your majestic power and glory. Open our eyes, that we may look unto Jesus, the Author and Finisher of our faith.

What happened to the servant? Suddenly his eyes were opened. He no longer saw the enemy's army. Instead, he saw the chariots of the Lord and the fire of God. He saw the angel of the Lord and the army of God surrounding them.

Only through prayer can we really be convinced that "They that be with us are more than they that be with them." When you have tasted of the power of prayer, you will not easily be discouraged. When situations get out of hand and circumstances move beyond your control, prayer will enable you to say:

Greater is he that is in you, than he that is in the world.
1 John 4:4

What shall we then say to these things? If God be for us, who can be against us?
Romans 8:31

The New Testament contains the accounts of the people of the early Church. These were people of prayer! In the first two chapters of the book of Acts, we find that one hundred and twenty disciples had gathered together in an upper room, and these men and women were devoting themselves to prayer (see Acts 1:14). As they prayed, they came into one accord. They were all in one place, their hearts were united, and they were agreeing together in prayer. So, what happened? The heavens were opened, and they received the Pentecostal experience. As the power of God came down in that room, they were all filled with the Holy Ghost and began to speak in tongues as the Spirit gave them utterance. The fire came down, the wind blew, and the nation heard it. It became a testimony, and three thousand souls were saved.

All of these things were the result of praying together in unity. They did not happen because of a seminar. There was no conference on how to receive the Holy Spirit. They had no manuals concerning the steps to follow to receive. These manifestations occurred because the believers were all in one accord, in one place, praying together in unity. Jesus said:

> *Again I say unto you, That if two of you shall agree on earth as touching any thing that they shall ask, it shall be done for them of my Father which is in heaven.* Matthew 18:19

> *Verily I say unto you, If ye have faith, and doubt not, ye shall not only do this which is done to the fig tree, but also if ye shall say unto this mountain, Be thou removed, and be thou cast into the sea; it shall be done.* Matthew 21:21

We read in Acts chapter 3 of the first miracle that took place in the early Church. Peter and John were going to the Temple *"at the hour of prayer, being the ninth hour"* (Acts 3:1). As they were on their way, they came across a lame man who was being carried every day to the Temple gate. There he would beg for alms. Seeing Peter and John, the man began to ask them for money, hoping for some coins.

> *And Peter, fastening his eyes upon him with John, said, Look on us. And he gave heed unto them, expecting to receive something of them. Then Peter said, Silver and gold have I none; but such as I have give I thee: In the name of Jesus Christ of Nazareth rise up and walk.* Acts 3:4-6

"I don't have any money, but I do have something better. I know how to pray. I know the God who answers prayer. So, in the name of Jesus Christ of Nazareth, rise up and walk!" And that is just what the man did. He started walking, and leaping, and praising God.

Many people are crippled spiritually, emotionally, or mentally. They are sitting around waiting for someone to come and feel sorry for them. If you are one of those people, then it's time to change. Release the power of prayer, and you will begin to walk and leap and sing praises to God.

If we continue to read about the early Church, we see that persecution set in. The high priest stirred up the Pharisees and the Sadducees to persecute the Church. So, what did the Church do? Instead of running to the mountains to find a hiding place, they ran to the One who could protect and defend them. They gathered together in prayer.

> *And when they had prayed, the place was shaken where they were assembled together; and they were all filled with the Holy Ghost, and they spake the word of God with boldness.* Acts 4:31

The place where those believers were praying was shaken. Beloved, we need to be shaken by the power of God! Then all things that need to be shaken will be shaken, and all what is needed will remain. The appetite of the flesh should be shaken. Pride should be shaken. Self-righteousness should be shaken. All that is not of God should be shaken until nothing is left except the glory, the presence, and power of God, and the righteousness of Jesus Christ. May the Church in this day be a praying Church, and may we be shaken by God.

Let's look to Acts 12. Here we read that James, the brother of John, has been killed by Herod. Since this pleased the Jews, Herod proceeded to arrest Peter and put him in jail. Four squads of soldiers were to guard him until after Passover, when Peter was to be brought out before the people and probably executed.

While Peter was in prison, the Church gathered together, and there was a solemn assembly of prayer and fasting on his behalf. While the Church was praying, Peter was sleeping. He was in a place of rest—even though he was chained between two guards. While Peter was sleeping and the Church was praying, the angel of the Lord made a surprise visit.

The angel of the Lord came to Peter's cell and woke him up. Suddenly the chains were released, the prison door was opened, and Peter walked out through the gate. He thought he was seeing a vision. It wasn't until he was on the street that he finally realized that these things were really happening.

Peter went to the place where the Church was meeting. Rhoda, a servant girl, heard him knocking. When she saw that it was Peter, she was so excited that she didn't even let him in. Instead, she rushed to tell the others. At first, they did not believe her; but then they came and saw for themselves that it was so.

Like us, these people simply could not comprehend the fact that God had answered their prayer. They could not believe that He had heard them. But whether you believe it or not, beloved, God hears and answers prayer. The ears of the Lord are open to the cry of the righteous. When you pray, He hears, and when He hears, He answers. Nothing is impossible with God.

In Acts 16, we find the beautiful story of Paul and Silas. These men of God were beaten and thrown in jail, where their hands and feet were placed in stocks. If this happened to us, how would we react? Fortunately, these two knew how to pray. They knew how to worship and praise the Lord God. As they began to pray and to worship, God came into that prison. He came to inhabit the praises and prayers of His people.

That jail had seen much human misery, it knew suffering, and it had stood aloof from it all, uncaring. But when the presence of the Lord filled that place of darkness and stench and the sound of chains and wails, then that jail was shaken! The chains were broken, and the doors flew open. The jailer was saved and was baptized in water. He and his family were brought into the Kingdom of God as a result of Paul and Silas' prayer in the midnight hour.

Do you want to see your household, your friends, your neighbors come to the Kingdom of God? Then, instead of looking at the situation, instead of seeing the wrong attitudes and the sins, begin to pray. Then keep them in prayer, and don't give up. The Lord is working even now. Because we cannot see all of the circumstances, we don't understand what God is doing. But that's all right, for we do know that He is at work. Prayer works!

CHAPTER 5

GOD'S VISION FOR PRAYER

And it came to pass, that, as he was praying in a certain place, when he ceased, one of his disciples said unto him, Lord, teach us to pray, as John also taught his disciples. Luke 11:1

The Church of our God is to be a praying Church, with each believer being a man or woman of prayer. Have you experienced prayer? Have you tasted of the goodness of God? Have you discovered the unlimited power of God when you have reached out to Him in prayer? Are you convinced, deep within your being, that God hears and answers prayer—your prayer?

A few years ago, a woman came to my office. She told me that she had lived a sinful lifestyle before coming to the Lord, and now she was reaping the consequences of her sin. Her doctor had diagnosed her as HIV-positive, but she had not come to me for prayer.

Oh, she had been praying. Whenever there was a time of prayer ministry at her church, she went forward to be prayed for, and people had been praying for her without knowing what her problem was. They simply prayed for her healing.

She said to me now, "Pastor, I want to make a report. That prayer is being answered." She explained that at one point her blood count was very low. The doctor had told her to continue taking her medication, but the Spirit told her, "Believe God."

She said that God had spoken to her and said, "If you believe Me, stop taking your medications." So she had stopped taking her medications even though her blood count was very low.

The doctor was angry with her. He said, "You're crazy! You'll die!"

But the woman replied that when she was taking the medications, she was losing weight and the symptoms were growing worse. She said, "If the medications are not working, why should I take them?" She had stopped the medications at the point when the symptoms were at their worst.

Soon, the symptoms disappeared, her appetite returned, and her blood count went up. It had now been two years since she had taken the medications, and she said, "Pastor, prayer works!" Amen! Nothing is impossible with God!

Prayer is a privilege that God has given to His people. It is also a necessity if we are to tap into the power of God for our lives and for those for whom we intercede. Prayer is to be a way of life, a way of thought, for the believer. But there is a basic question we must ask before we can continue: what is prayer?

First, prayer involves belief:

> *But the ship was now in the midst of the sea, tossed with waves: for the wind was contrary. And in the fourth watch of the night Jesus went unto them, walking on the sea. And when the disciples saw him walking on the sea, they were troubled, saying, It is a spirit; and they cried out for fear. But straightway Jesus spake unto them, saying, Be of good cheer; it is I; be not afraid. And Peter answered him and said, Lord, if it be thou, bid me come unto thee on the water. ...* Matthew 14:24-28

Peter's prayer was answered right away. The Lord said, *"Come."* Peter believed that his prayer had been heard and answered, so he got up and stepped out of the boat.

How do you suppose the other disciples responded to that?

"Oh brother! Peter, can't you see that's water?
You must not be too bright!"
"Do you have a fever? Maybe you're delirious."
"Touch it. It feels like water. It smells like water. Drink it. It
tastes like water. That's water!"
"Do you think it can hold you up? Let us tell you about the
laws of nature. You will go under!"

But Peter only heard one word, *"Come,"* and then he began to act on his prayer. He stepped out of the boat. "I'm coming, Lord!"

We need to have this type of faith! When we hear God telling us to do something, we must do it. Not only will we begin to see ourselves being used of the Lord in ministry to others; but, as we obey what the Lord has said, we will grow in God and in hearing the word of the Lord in our spirits.

When we pray, we need first to verbalize our prayer. Then we need to visualize our prayer. This simply means that we need to see with eyes of faith. We are to look to see what God is doing in the lives of those for whom we are praying.

After verbalizing and visualizing our prayers, we need to actualize them. This means we need to act on them. If God has given us the burden to pray for someone or something, then He will often use us to work His will for good in that situation. We can talk to people, share with them, pray with them, and minister to their practical needs. As we open ourselves to the possibilities of ministering to others and as we spend time in the presence of the Lord, learning to hear and recognize His voice, God will be able to speak to us more and more often and more and more clearly.

So, first, if we are to pray effectively, we need to have faith:

But without faith it is impossible to please him: for he that cometh to God must believe that he is, and that he is a rewarder of them that diligently seek him. Hebrews 11:6

If we have faith that God exists and that He will reward those who seek Him, we are ready to begin to pray.

At its simplest, prayer is communicating with God. But there are several facets of this that we can explore. First, I believe that prayer is seeking God:

But if from thence thou shalt seek the LORD thy God, thou shalt find him, if thou seek him with all thy heart and with all thy soul. Deuteronomy 4:29

Then shall ye call upon me, and ye shall go and pray unto me, and I will hearken unto you. And ye shall seek me, and find me, when ye shall search for me with all your heart. And I will be found of you, saith the LORD. Jeremiah 29:12-14

When you seek God in prayer with all your heart and with all your soul, you will find Him, for He has promised that it will be so. And when you find God, you will find the answer to your need. When you find God, you will find the miracles that you are seeking. When you find God, you will find the blessings of the Lord. Yes, we find all that we need when we seek God in prayer.

But what do I mean by "seeking God"? I mean that you should pray and pray fervently. I mean that you should lay your problem or your need before the Lord and ask Him to supply the answers. I mean that you should look first to Him and not to your own abilities or strengths. I mean that you should come to the Lord, trusting in His love, as well as in His power.

This kind of prayer is like a little girl whose mother has gone out for a time. When the mother returns, the child runs to her, flinging herself into her mother's arms. She is so excited to see her mother! Prayer is somewhat like that. It is seeking God, pursuing God, running after Him. In prayer, we come closer to God, finding our way into His presence.

When you seek God in prayer, you are bringing yourself into proper alignment with God so that you are in a position to receive His favor. You must know that when your car is not properly aligned, it will not run smoothly. When I first learned how to drive, I didn't know much about cars. I said to a friend, "Why does my car keep pulling to the right?"

He answered, "Your car needs alignment."

Many people, instead of walking straight into the presence and provision of God, are out of alignment. They miss their goal. They are out of alignment with God, and so they are continually pulling off to the right or to the left, working to fulfill their own desires, and not seeking after the will of the Lord. Prayer is what brings us into alignment with God. Prayer, seeking the counsel and the wisdom of God, allows us to say with Solomon:

Trust in the LORD with all thine heart; and lean not unto thine own understanding. In all thy ways acknowledge him, and he shall direct thy paths.   Proverbs 3:5-6

Is your life in alignment with God? Or are you still walking in your own paths? Our problem is that we like to go our own way ... until we have completely exhausted ourselves, doing everything we can do in our own ability and might. Then we remember God. What an insult to God this is! Don't make God your last resort; make Him your first resource. Go straight to His paths of righteousness, knowing that He is your Refuge and Strength:

But seek ye first the kingdom of God, and his righteousness; and all these things shall be added unto you.   Matthew 6:33

Yes, seek Him first.

Noah was a man who was righteous in the sight of God. The Bible says, *"Noah found grace in the eyes of the LORD"* (Genesis 6:8). In other words, Noah found favor with God; He became pleasing to God. When you have found favor with the Lord, you have overcome your fear and anxiety concerning Him. Then you are in a place of rest and peace, tranquility and joy. But if you don't have God's favor, then watch out! You will be filled with anxiety and fear, stress and unrest. It is very important to have favor with God. This is what we were created for.

When you have found favor with someone, it puts you into a position of grace. You are relaxed, with nothing to worry about while you are in that person's presence.

Ray Llarena

Back in December of 1973, I was riding a bus from Philadelphia to Baltimore, which was quite a long ride. I had just finished preaching at a ten-day series of revival meetings. I had been up late every night of those meetings, and I was exhausted. I climbed onto the bus, relieved that I could sleep through the journey. I was seated in the third row from the front, and I had just settled in to rest when the Spirit of the Lord said to me, "Preach." This is a form of evangelism that we often employ in the Philippines, but I said, "Lord, I'm tired. I have no more strength." So I leaned over toward the window and tried to go to sleep.

But again the Spirit of the Lord said, "Preach."

I looked around at the other passengers. I was the only foreigner on the bus. I was also the smallest man on the bus. I tried to ignore the Spirit, but you can only ignore that voice for so long. If you are a born-again believer and if you commune with God in prayer regularly, then you cannot continue to resist Him. You are compelled to obey His voice.

I decided to obey the Lord. I turned to the people behind me, two distinguished looking, well-dressed businessmen. They were discussing President Nixon and Watergate, the current events at the time. When I heard that, I jumped into the conversation. They were speaking of how Nixon had been caught, and I said, "You know, that is very scriptural: *'Be sure your sin will find you out,'* " and I began to preach.

As I preached, someone at the back of the bus was saying, "Where is that voice coming from?" They couldn't see me. At that, I became afraid.

But the driver turned off the radio, and when he turned it off, I looked up at him. Our eyes met, and he smiled at me and nodded his head. When I saw that, I thought, "Praise God! I've found favor here!" I preached from that moment until we pulled into the bus depot at Baltimore.

Finding favor with that driver really blessed me. I had someone else to back me up. As long as the driver, who was in charge of the bus, looked on me with favor, I was free to preach. He was not going to tell me to be quiet, and he was not going to put me off the bus.

I also found favor with some of the other passengers, who encouraged me as I preached. I learned that the two businessmen were Baptist believers. By the time we reached Baltimore, although I did not asked for anything, a blessing came to me. My fellow passengers gave me enough money to cover all my expenses for a time, with some extra pocket money.

Seek the Lord and find the favor of God. Come into a position where God will smile upon you rather than being angry with you. When you cultivate a spirit of prayer, you are aligning yourself with the Lord, putting yourself in a posture of blessing and obedience, and you will find the favor of God.

Sometimes we pray, but we are not in tune with God. We say words, and we are determined, but we are not seeing any results. Why is that? Usually it is because we are not in proper harmony with God. When you seek God with all your heart, it will bring you into a place of union and agreement with Him. You will no longer be rebellious or stubborn, but will delight in submitting to God and to His will for you. This is part of finding His favor.

Sometimes we seek the favor of men. That is understandable, but it is also much less important than seeking God's favor and approval. Men are very fickle. Even if you gain the approval of men, how long will it last? What will it benefit you? Where will you be when that favor has passed from you and is being given to someone else?

Instead, beloved, when you are in need, seek the Lord. If you have a bigger need, you must have a stronger faith. Pray and find God's favor. You will never know true security or real peace until you have sought the Lord and found Him. When you discover that God is for you and not against you, that He has plans for good and not for evil in your life, then you will be able to lean upon Him in trust and be at peace.

I have visited many offices through the years, seeking favor for help with certain projects. I can recall many times when I left those offices disappointed, disheartened, and defeated. But God does not fail us. When you come before the Lord in prayer with an honest, sincere heart and you seek Him with all your might, all your strength, all your soul, and all your spirit, then God will open the windows of Heaven, and you will see His face smiling upon you. You will enter into the favor of God, for God's heart is always with those who seek Him.

The Lord God gave Moses a blessing for Aaron and his sons to speak over Israel:

> *The LORD bless thee, and keep thee: the LORD make his face shine upon thee, and be gracious unto thee: the LORD lift up his countenance upon thee, and give thee peace.*   Numbers 6:24-26

I believe that as we seek God in prayer, this blessing will be ours as well. As the face of the Lord shines upon you, you will come to know His favor. You will see that God is glad when He can bless you and minister to you.

How do you respond when you face a time that seems to be filled to overflowing with difficulties? The next time this happens, rather than feeling sorry for yourself—grumbling, murmuring, and becoming sour in your spirit because of your predicament— seek the Lord. Seek His favor. When you find the favor of the Lord, beloved, you will never be the same:

> *Glory ye in his holy name: let the heart of them rejoice that seek*
> *the Lord. Seek the Lord, and his strength: seek his face evermore.*
>   Psalm 105:3-4

When you are weak, you look for help from someone who is stronger than you. When you are financially burdened, you look for someone for guidance who is more financially stable than you. When you are going through times of pain, heartache and sorrow, you look for someone to comfort you who has already come through such times. But no matter how long or how hard you may look, you will never find anyone as strong, as wise, or as perfect as God.

His Word to us is sure. As you pray, recall to your mind the promises of God. Are you in need? Then remember His Word that is filled with promise:

> *But my God shall supply all your need according to his riches in*
> *glory by Christ Jesus.*   Philippians 4:19

When you are weak, meditate on His words to you:

> *And he said unto me, My grace is sufficient for thee: for my*
> *strength is made perfect in weakness. Most gladly therefore will*

I rather glory in my infirmities, that the power of Christ may rest upon me. 2 Corinthians 12:9

When you walk in the darkness of suffering, temptation, or despair, remember that Christ is our Light:

Then spake Jesus again unto them, saying, I am the light of the world: he that followeth me shall not walk in darkness, but shall have the light of life. John 8:12

We have nothing to fear when we know God. He is as close as a prayer. Seek Him with all your heart.

Sometimes we make God our last resort rather than our first resource. We look for help from everyone we can find first. Then, after we have been disappointed by all to whom we turn, we remember God. Then we begin to pray. But prayer is a privilege and an opportunity. God has made that door for us so that when we have needs, we can come to Him in favor and may seek Him with all our heart.

Seek ye the LORD while he may be found, call ye upon him while he is near ... . Isaiah 55:6

God is near to you, beloved. He is not just at hand; He dwells within your heart, your very being. Therefore, the favor of God is in you, the power of God is in you, and the beauty of God is in you. God is close to you, closer than the breath in your body. The Bible says, *"In him we live and move and have our being"* (Acts 17:28). We live in the presence of God. We move in the presence of God.

We exist in the presence of God. Without Him, we can do nothing. What did Christ promise to those who were His followers?

> *Teaching them to observe all things whatsoever I have commanded you: and, lo, I am with you alway, even unto the end of the world. Amen.*   Matthew 28:20

Jesus did not promise to be with us "sometimes," or "often," but *"alway[s]."* We are not just God's hobby — something He does in His spare time. He is with you constantly, and He will never leave you. He will be with you even through your struggles, your sorrows, and your difficulties. He will be there, even though you may not see Him at first. But when you seek Him, you will find Him.

Some people try to drink their misery away. Others use drugs. Still others use television or food. But the Bible tells us that we can turn to God:

> *Sow to yourselves in righteousness, reap in mercy; break up your fallow ground: for it is time to seek the LORD, till he come and rain righteousness upon you.*   Hosea 10:12

What time is it? It's time to seek the Lord. When is it time to pray? Right now. Sometimes we pray only when we have needs, because we have a poor concept of prayer. We think of it only in terms of what we can receive. But there is so much more to prayer than that!

Prayer is worship, thanksgiving, praise. Yes, there are prayers of supplication, of petition, and of intercession, but there are also prayers of thanksgiving and of adoration. It's time to seek the Lord. It's time to know God's favor, time to come into harmony with God.

You can never win by fighting God. You'll never know blessing or victory by resisting God. Instead, give in to Him. Surrender your life to Him. Say, "Here am I, Lord. I am seeking You with all my heart." As you pray, remember His promise to those who seek: *"You shall find him."*

So prayer is seeking God, but there are other definitions too. I believe that prayer also includes a sincere, honest, positive, truthful attitude. It is not hypocritical or self-righteous. When you pray, you are pouring out your soul unto God through the help and assistance of the Holy Spirit. Prayer must reflect the truthfulness and sincerity of your heart before God, your honesty in accepting the fact that you have a need that is beyond your ability to meet. One who prays with a pure heart does not try to cover or hide his inability; he brings it to God, knowing that:

> [God] *is able to do exceeding abundantly above all that we ask or think, according to the power that worketh in us.*
>
> Ephesians 3:20

Prayer involves opening your spirit and unashamedly crying out to God. We can be honest with the Lord, knowing that it truly is His power that works within us. We don't need to rely on our own strength.

How do you respond when people ask, "How are you?" You may say, "Wonderful! Great! I'm blessed," But inside you are miserable and dying. What does that make you? A hypocrite. But you cannot respond that way to God. Oh, you can try. But if you have an active and vital prayer life, you cannot continue to put Him off. He already knows the truth anyway.

Prayer will change us. It will make us honest before God. It will make us truthful and sincere before the Lord. As we live in an attitude of prayer, we will learn to love the Lord more. We will be more open before Him, because we will know and experience the truth, that there is nothing we can hide from the eyes of God. He knows the number of the hairs on your head. He sees how the bills are piling up on your table. There is nothing that you can hide from God. He sees you in the light and in the darkness. There is no place you can go to hide from the Lord:

> *Whither shall I go from thy spirit? or whither shall I flee from thy presence? If I ascend up into heaven, thou art there: if I make my bed in hell, behold, thou art there. If I take the wings of the morning, and dwell in the uttermost parts of the sea; even there shall thy hand lead me, and thy right hand shall hold me.*
>
> Psalm 139:7-10

You cannot hide from God. You might as well face that reality and come into a position of harmony with Him. Begin to pour out your soul to God, whether it is with bitter tears and anguish of your spirit or with songs and psalms of thanksgiving and praise. Seek Him with all your heart, because the remedy, the answer, the miracle, the provision is in the hand of God.

Prayer is not just a ritual in which you mumble some words. It is the attitude and condition of the heart. Prayer is not merely a matter of repeating the right phrases, nor is it to be found in the position of your body. You can kneel or be seated, stand or walk. The position of your body is not important; the position of your heart is.

Do you recall how Elijah faced the prophets of Baal? After God had been proven the true God, Elijah saw that it was time for the rain to come again to the land. It had been stopped by the Lord at the proclamation of the prophet because of the sin of the people. But now that they had acknowledged the true and living God, the rain of blessing could come once again:

> *And Elijah said unto Ahab, Get thee up, eat and drink; for there is a sound of abundance of rain. So Ahab went up to eat and to drink.* 1 Kings 18:41-42

Elijah looked to God, and what did he see? Blessing was coming. Prosperity was coming. Deliverance was on its way. There was only one obstacle: the beautiful, bright, clear blue sky of a sunny day.

So Elijah went to the top of Mount Carmel, to the pinnacle of the mountain of God's proving before Israel. There he *"cast himself down upon the earth, and put his face between his knees"* (verse 42). Elijah needed to pray. If the rain did not come, the king would probably punish him.

I believe that Elijah began to pour out his soul before God. He did not look to the situation, and he did not magnify the condition. Instead, he opened the very reservoir of his spirit to God without holding back. He released everything to God. Then he turned to his servant.

"Go up into the mountain,: he said, "look toward the sea and tell me whether the clouds are coming."

The servant went to look. When he returned, he said, "No, there is nothing."

"Go and look again," Elijah commanded. Then, while the servant went to look, the prophet continued to pray. The more he poured out his soul to the Lord, the more the pride came out, the self-righteousness, the self-confidence. As he prayed, he felt purified. His faith was revived. The righteousness of God came to the surface, and Elijah became strong in the revelation of the knowledge of God.

Elijah had the servant go to look again seven times:

And it came to pass at the seventh time, that he said, Behold, there ariseth a little cloud out of the sea, like a man's hand. And he said, Go up, say unto Ahab, Prepare thy chariot, and get thee down, that the rain stop thee not.
And it came to pass in the mean while, that the heaven was black with clouds and wind, and there was a great rain. And Ahab rode, and went to Jezreel. And the hand of the LORD was on Elijah; and he girded up his loins, and ran before Ahab to the entrance of Jezreel. 1 Kings 18:44-46

Put everything in the hands of God. He operates beyond our logic, beyond our intellect, beyond our knowledge and beyond our understanding. As a matter of fact, these are all things that can stand against faith. Prayer cannot be rationalized. You cannot put prayer into a system of logic. When you pray, you move from the realm of men's logic to that of the supernatural.

Elijah was in that supernatural realm, for the hand of God was upon him. He ran faster than the horses of Ahab, back to the city of Jezreel. He had prayed and now he was energized by the power of God. Therefore, he could do things that he could not otherwise have done. The same can be true of us as well, for we serve a supernatural God.

Give yourself to prayer. Taste and see that the Lord is good. Know that His goodness endures forever. Just as oxygen is necessary to the lungs, so is prayer necessary to your spirit and soul. Prayer is the breath of your soul and your spirit. When you stop praying, you die. Sometimes, just as in the physical world, you can receive CPR, as when someone comes to revive a person who has stopped breathing. But isn't it far better to remain healthy? Let prayer be your source of spiritual health.

What is prayer? It is a virtue that prevails against all temptation. If you are a prayerful person, temptation will not so easily have victory over you. Too often, the reason we are overcome by temptation is that we don't know to pray. Prayer is the key to the power of God. When temptations come, link yourself to that Source of power. Through prayer, you can touch God's heart, and He will give you the ability to overcome every temptation—the lust of the flesh, the lust of the eyes, and the pride of life.

Prayer, the prayer that comes from a faith-filled spirit, crowns God with honor and glory. How often do we pray, not believing that our prayer will be answered? That's an insult to God! "Why did you come and ask Me something when you didn't believe I would do it for you?" He is saying. It's a disgrace to God. But when you begin to pray in faith, you are crowning Him with honor and glory, showing that there is no one like our God. There is nothing impossible with Him, for our God is supreme, eternal, and all-powerful. Prayer crowns God with the honor and glory due His name.

In return, God crowns prayer with the assurance and comfort that the one who prays will receive whatever his soul asks for. In other words, prayer will put God in the place where He should be, and prayer will put you in the place you should be. What does the Bible tell us?

> *Again I say unto you, That if two of you shall agree on earth as touching any thing that they shall ask, it shall be done for them of my Father which is in heaven. For where two or three are gathered together in my name, there am I in the midst of them.* Matthew 18:19-20

When you come into agreement with God, you are in harmony with Him, you are in a proper position with Him, and you can pray in agreement with Him.

Finally, prayer is intimacy with God. Prayer is talking with God, but it can go much deeper. Prayer is having a sweet communion, an intimacy, with our Creator. As marriage will bring a man and a woman into an intimate relationship wherein they will become one flesh, so prayer will bring a man or woman, boy or girl into an intimate relationship with God. Prayer allows us to see God with the eyes of our soul:

> *Beloved, now are we the sons of God, and it doth not yet appear what we shall be: but we know that, when he shall appear, we shall be like him; for we shall see him as he is. And every*

man that hath this hope in him purifieth himself, even as he
is pure.   1 John 3:2-3

As we look to God, we are changed more and more into His image and likeness. That is how we come into agreement with Him, and that is how we build intimacy with Him.

Come away, beloved, and pray.

CHAPTER 6

THE VISION FOR PRAYER BECOMES OUR MISSION

And when he [Jesus] had sent the multitudes away, he went up
into a mountain apart to pray: and when the evening was come,
he was there alone.   Matthew 14:23

Prayer is a gift from the Lord to His people. He has given us this means of knowing Him, of experiencing His presence, of growing in Him, of communicating with Him. Thank God for this precious gift!

But sometimes we have difficulties with the concept of prayer. After all, isn't God all-knowing? If He knows my need, why should I have to tell Him about it? If God wants to bless me, He can do so without me asking Him, since He already knows what it is that I would ask.

Yes, God is all-knowing, but what we need to realize is that our prayer is not for the sake of God; it's for our own sake:

Ask, and it shall be given you; seek, and ye shall find; knock, and
it shall be opened unto you: for every one that asketh receiveth;
and he that seeketh findeth; and to him that knocketh it shall be
opened.   Matthew 7:7-8

There is power in prayer. If we simply wait for the Lord to meet our needs, we will not know this power. Nor will we be able to use it, either to meet the needs in our own lives or on behalf of others. Sadly, there are many people who have lived in the Kingdom for a long time, yet have never really experienced the power of prayer. He who is a stranger to prayer is a stranger to the power of God. He who doesn't know how to pray doesn't truly know God.

If you know God in a very intimate, personal way, it will drive you to Him in prayer. God allows our needs and our circumstances, and also persecutions and trials to come into our lives. Nothing can touch us that He has not allowed. But why does He permit these things? I believe that, sometimes, it is so that we may be stirred to prayer. Sometimes we have to clearly see a need or a lack in our lives before we will begin to pray.

So why should we pray? First, because prayer, like evangelism, is a command from God. A command needs to be obeyed. If you ask your child to do something and he does not do it, then you recognize that it is time for discipline. Why? Because you want your children to be obedient to you. You want them to listen to you and to heed what you say. You want your children to follow your instructions.

Prayer is a command from God, and since it is a command, there is no alternative but to follow, to obey, and to pursue. Let us not be rebellious toward the Word of God. When the Lord says, "Pray," we must listen. We must obey. We must pray.

Seek the LORD and his strength, seek his face continually.
1 Chronicles 16:11

How often should we seek His face? How long should we seek Him? *"Continually."* Please notice that this verse is written in the form of a command. This is not just a good idea; it is a command from the Lord. We are to seek Him continually, in good times and bad times, in times of blessing and in times of barrenness. We need to seek the Lord.

The American Church in general seems to have a very poor concept of prayer. Our idea of prayer is, "Give me, give me, give me! Bless me, bless me, bless me! Heal me, heal me, heal me!" Most of our prayer is centered on ourselves, our problems, our families or our own narrow worlds. This is a selfish type of prayer.

But we know that there are different kinds of prayer: intercession, supplication, thanksgiving, repentance, adoration. We can name various kinds of prayer. We are not commanded to pray just one specific type of prayer; we are commanded to pray.

After we receive the answer to our supplication or our intercession, we need to respond with a prayer of thanksgiving. Our response should be a time of rejoicing in the Lord for hearing our prayer, for answering us, and for ministering to us in our time of need:

Thus saith the LORD; *Cursed be the man that trusteth in man, and maketh flesh his arm, and whose heart departeth from the* LORD. *For he shall be like the heath in the desert, and shall not see when good cometh; but shall inhabit the parched places in the wilderness, in a salt land and not inhabited. Blessed is the man that trusteth in the* LORD, *and whose hope the* LORD *is. For he shall be as a tree planted by the waters, and that spreadeth out her roots by the river, and shall not see when heat cometh, but her leaf shall be green; and shall not be careful in the year of drought, neither shall cease from yielding fruit.*   Jeremiah 17:5-8

Trust in the Lord! Bring your concerns to Him. Don't look to man or to the plans of men; look to the Lord and trust in His counsel. It is better to trust in the Lord than to put confidence in the flesh—even your own flesh. We cannot always trust our own "common sense." We must look to the Lord.

Ask! Seek! Knock! If you are not receiving, perhaps it is because you are not asking. If you are not finding, perhaps it is because you are not seeking. And if the door is not opening to you, perhaps it is that you are not knocking.

Christ gave the example of a man who was faithful to continue in his knocking, seeking, and asking, until finally he received that which he lacked:

> *And he said unto them, Which of you shall have a friend, and shall go unto him at midnight, and say unto him, Friend, lend me three loaves; for a friend of mine in his journey is come to me, and I have nothing to set before him? And he from within shall answer and say, Trouble me not: the door is now shut, and my children are with me in bed; I cannot rise and give thee. I say unto you, Though he will not rise and give him, because he is his friend, yet because of his importunity he will rise and give him as many as he needeth. And I say unto you, Ask, and it shall be given you; seek, and ye shall find; knock, and it shall be opened unto you.* Luke 11:5-9

This man kept on seeking. He kept on knocking. He kept on asking. Eventually, he received his heart's desire. It is interesting to note that this instruction immediately follows Christ's teaching to His disciples on what we know as The Lord's Prayer. This example directly relates to prayer:

> *Watch and pray, that ye enter not into temptation: the spirit indeed is willing, but the flesh is weak.*   Matthew 26:41

The context of this verse is the Garden of Gethsemane, just before Jesus was betrayed by Judas Iscariot. In the midst of great personal turmoil, Jesus commanded His followers to watch and pray. What does this mean?

We are to be alert when we pray. Many Christians have fallen into temptation because they were not watchful. Most of our problems are not caused by the devil; they are caused by our own spiritual carelessness. We grow lazy and careless in our spiritual life, and we neglect watchfulness. When you know there is an enemy about, you need to be watching at all times. So, watch and pray. Do not neglect this commandment from God.

Nehemiah gives us a picture of this watchful stance. He was leading the people of Israel in the rebuilding of the wall around Jerusalem after their destruction and captivity. But the kings and peoples around them were not happy about this. They wanted Jerusalem to remain the pile of ruins to which it had been reduced:

> *But when Sanballat the Horonite, and Tobiah the servant, the Ammonite, and Geshem the Arabian, heard it, they laughed us to scorn, and despised us, and said, What is this thing that ye do? will ye rebel against the king?*   Nehemiah 2:19

When their mockings did not stop the work of rebuilding, the enemies of Israel turned to battle:

> *But it came to pass, that when Sanballat, and Tobiah, and the Arabians, and the Ammonites, and the Ashdodites, heard that the walls of Jerusalem were made up, and that the breaches began to be stopped, then they were very wroth, and conspired all of them together to come and to fight against Jerusalem, and to hinder it. Nevertheless we made our prayer unto our God, and set a watch against them day and night, because of them.*
>
> Nehemiah 4:7-9

"Nevertheless we made our prayer unto our God." In time of trouble, Israel prayed to God. Nehemiah did not halt the work simply because Israel's enemies were coming to attack them as they built. Instead, he trusted in the Lord God. He and the people watched and prayed:

> *And it came to pass, when our enemies heard that it was known unto us, and God had brought their counsel to nought, that we returned all of us to the wall, every one unto his work. And it came to pass from that time forth, that the half of my servants wrought in the work, and the other half of them held both the spears, the shields, and the bows, and the habergeons; and the rulers were behind all the house of Judah. They which builded on the wall, and they that bare burdens, with those that laded, every one with one of his hands wrought in the work, and with the other hand held a weapon.*
>
> Nehemiah 4:15-17

These builders were working. They were steadfastly continuing the task they had been given to do. They were faithful to what the Lord was requiring of them for that time. At the same time, they were watching. They were concentrating, focusing, looking to make sure that the enemy could not gain any foothold to disrupt the work God had given them.

Many of us don't seem to know how to watch. We lack focus. Instead of concentrating steadfastly, our minds are wandering. What are we to focus on?

Looking unto Jesus the author and finisher of our faith; who for the joy that was set before him endured the cross, despising the shame, and is set down at the right hand of the throne of God. For consider him that endured such contradiction of sinners against himself, lest ye be wearied and faint in your minds.

Hebrews 12:2-3

Look unto Jesus. Fix your eyes upon Him, consider Him, focus your attention on Him. Reach out to Christ Jesus by faith. And be faithful to watch as you pray.

Besides being watchful, our prayer is also to be one of faith. Christ promised:

Hitherto have ye asked nothing in my name: ask, and ye shall receive, that your joy may be full. John 16:24

When you are in need, it is difficult to rejoice. It is hard to be glad in the Lord when the bills are mounting, when relationships fail, or when illness strikes. When you face such difficult times, turn to the Lord. After all, your prayers cannot be answered if you have not prayed.

Commune with God. Fellowship with Him. Come to know Him in a relational way. Once you have come to Him in prayer, allowing His heart to touch yours, you will never again be the same. When you come forth from the presence of the Lord, you will no longer be the same person; you will become a glory-bearer, one who bears the presence of the Lord, that you may share it with others. You will be changed, transformed by the power of God:

> *Praying always with all prayer and supplication in the Spirit, and watching thereunto with all perseverance and supplication for all saints.* Ephesians 6:18

> *Pray without ceasing.* 1 Thessalonians 5:17

How often do we need to pray? *"Continually," "without ceasing."* That's a lot of prayer! Pray every time you have a need, every time you have a praise, every time you want to open yourself to be used by God in a given situation. We are to continually be in fellowship with our Lord.

It isn't always enough to pray once concerning a situation. Sometimes we need to persevere in our prayer:

> *And he* [Christ Jesus] *spake a parable unto them to this end, that men ought always to pray, and not to faint; saying, There was in a city a judge, which feared not God, neither regarded man: and there was a widow in that city; and she came unto him, saying, Avenge me of mine adversary. And he would not for a while: but*

afterward he said within himself, Though I fear not God, nor regard man; yet because this widow troubleth me, I will avenge her, lest by her continual coming she weary me. And the LORD said, Hear what the unjust judge saith. And shall not God avenge his own elect, which cry day and night unto him, though he bear long with them? I tell you that he will avenge them speedily. Nevertheless when the Son of man cometh, shall he find faith on the earth?   Luke 18:1-8

If an ungodly judge can do what is right for a widow, how much more will our heavenly Father do for His beloved children?

He that spared not his own Son, but delivered him up for us all, how shall he not with him also freely give us all things?
                                        Romans 8:32

If a son shall ask bread of any of you that is a father, will he give him a stone? or if he ask a fish, will he for a fish give him a serpent? Or if he shall ask an egg, will he offer him a scorpion? If ye then, being evil, know how to give good gifts unto your children: how much more shall your heavenly Father give the Holy Spirit to them that ask him?   Luke 11:11-13

How generous is our God! He pours forth His blessing from the abundance of His love upon all those who fear His name. Our part is to keep our hearts pure before Him. As we seek Him, we are changed, so that His desires become our desires, and we seek after the glory of God on the earth.

How do we come to this level of relationship? *"Pray without ceasing."* Does this mean we should all quit our jobs, sit at home without eating or sleeping, and pray? Of course not! A Sunday school teacher once asked her class, "What would you do if I asked you to pray nonstop?"

One little girl said, "I would do what my mamma usually does."

"What does your mamma do?" she asked.

"She prays all the time. Even when she is sleeping, she is still praying. When she is cleaning the house, she says, 'You know what is in my heart. As this vacuum cleaner is cleaning this rug, vacuum away everything that is in my heart that is not supposed to be there.' When she is washing the dishes, she says, 'As the soap washes all the grease from this plate, may all the grease and dirt in my life of the flesh be washed away.' When she is ironing the clothes, she says, 'Lord, please let every wrinkle in my life be ironed and be pressed and be removed.' "

That's nonstop praying. We can be in an attitude of prayer continually when we obey the command of the Lord, "Watch and pray." If you are driving, put on some praise music and begin to worship the Lord. If you are working at a computer, ask God's help with your task and then begin to thank Him and praise Him. If you are cooking your meals or doing the laundry, you can be praying. Prayer is not only the words we speak; it is the attitude of the heart. Why? Because God is everywhere present.

Why should we pray? Because we are always in need of God's help. It may be physical, it may be financial, and it certainly is spiritual. We never outgrow our need of God. Yet our needs are as nothing compared to the knowledge of the glory of our God. They are not worth mentioning compared to the power of His majestic glory that is available to us. Our needs are as nothing compared to the everlasting promises of God.

Our needs will never end, but God doesn't end either. Our needs will continue to press upon us, but our God will consistently bring provision for His people.

When the Lord raised up Moses to lead His people out of Egypt, they didn't seem to be able to learn this lesson. All they had known was slavery, and provision for their needs was something new to them:

> *And when they came to Marah, they could not drink of the waters of Marah, for they were bitter: therefore the name of it was called Marah. And the people murmured against Moses, saying, What shall we drink?* Exodus 15:23-24

The startling aspect of this passage is that a mere two verses before this, Israel was praising God for bringing them across the Red Sea and for the victory over Pharaoh! According to verse 22, they were only a three-day journey into the wilderness at this point. The power of God had just delivered them from the Egyptians. Yet when they arrived at Marah and found no water to drink, the people began to murmur and complain.

That's human nature. There will always be an abundance of things to complain about, but we don't have to live that way. We need not be bound to such an outlook on life. We can determine within our hearts that we will focus on our God, not on those things which disappoint or frustrate us. We can determine to major in praise and thanksgiving, not in murmuring and complaining.

When you begin to complain, you become carnal. Complaining places you squarely in the realm of the flesh. I have determined that I will no longer complain. I will still speak forth on issues that need to be addressed, but I will not complain. You can make that decision too.

Murmuring and complaining are signs of rebellion, whether you realize it or not. God requires that His people submit to Him and to His will for our lives. When we learn to totally submit our lives to God, then there is nothing to complain about. When you submit to God, He is in control. And when God is in control, things will be different. It is when we try to be in control that things go from bad to worse.

Let's see how the Lord responded to Israel's need:

And he [Moses] *cried unto the LORD; and the LORD showed him a tree, which when he had cast into the waters, the waters were made sweet: there he made for them a statute and an ordinance, and there he proved them.*   Exodus 15:25

Fortunately for the children of Israel, Moses did not join in with their complaining. There was one person at Marah who chose to look to the Lord. There was one man who prayed. Moses knew that when there was a need, there would also be a provision. And God did not fail him.

If you walk a bitter path, lay hold of the promises of God. Cast those promises into the troubled waters of your life, and watch them become sweet. If you murmur and complain about your lot, then your situation will become even more bitter. But if you allow your attitude to be changed, if you determine to walk in the sweetness of praise and thanksgiving, looking unto God and taking Him at His Word, then will you begin to see the sweetness of God permeate your life.

You don't need to run from meeting to meeting, from counselor to counselor, from prophet to prophet. Learn to come to the Lord in prayer. Learn to hear His voice, and He will tell you what to do. Then, when a prophet speaks a word to you, he will confirm what God has already spoken to your heart.

When you are troubled, don't turn to man; turn first to God. Allow Him to bring those people to you who will minister from His heart to your situation.

The book of 1 Samuel tells of one woman who trusted God and did not allow man to dissuade her from seeking after God. Here name was Hannah, and she was barren in a time and a place where children were a measure of a woman's worth. She went with her husband to Shiloh year by year to sacrifice to God, and while she was there, she sought the Lord:

> *And she was in bitterness of soul, and prayed unto the LORD and wept sore. And she vowed a vow, and said, O LORD of hosts, if thou wilt indeed look on the affliction of thine handmaid, and remember me, and not forget thine handmaid, but wilt give unto thine handmaid a man child, then I will give him unto the LORD all the days of his life, and there shall no razor come upon his head.* 1 Samuel 1:10-11

As Hannah was seeking God, man tried to interfere:

> *And it came to pass, as she continued praying before the LORD, that Eli marked her mouth. Now Hannah, she spake in her heart;*

only her lips moved, but her voice was not heard: therefore Eli thought she had been drunken. And Eli said unto her, How long wilt thou be drunken? put away thy wine from thee.

1 Samuel 1:12-14

Hannah had to explain her heaviness of heart to the priest Eli before he would bless her. Many people will not understand your trials or sufferings, but the Lord always understands.

When your heart is heavy, don't talk to your friends; talk to God. When you are confused, don't talk to your friends about the matter; they will only confuse you further. Instead, talk to God. When you are in need of direction, don't turn to man. Go to God first. He will bring people across your path who will bring you clarity of direction.

The Lord blessed Hannah's seeking, gave her a son, and she brought her son to serve in the Temple, just as she had promised. This was her testimony to Eli:

And she said, Oh my lord, as thy soul liveth, my lord, I am the woman that stood by thee here, praying unto the LORD. For this child I prayed; and the LORD hath given me my petition which I asked of him. 1 Samuel 1:26-17

Why do we need to pray? Because God promised that He will answer us if and when we pray:

Call unto me, and I will answer thee, and show thee great and mighty things, which thou knowest not. Jeremiah 33:3

He shall call upon me, and I will answer him: I will be with him in trouble; I will deliver him, and honour him.   Psalm 91:15

Then shalt thou call, and the LORD shall answer; thou shalt cry, and he shall say, Here I am.   Isaiah 58:9a

"The LORD will answer." Do you really believe that? But how can He answer you if you don't call on Him? And if you know He will answer, why do you not call out to Him?

You may say, "But the Lord knows already my need." Yes, He does know your need. But He wants to teach you to act in faith and obedience. He intends that His children learn to apply the provision of His promises. He wants you to learn to take His word seriously and to obey it.

Finally, we need to consider one more area—conditions. God will not grant our every petition. He will not be manipulated by our prayers or our logic. There are conditions to be met, if we want God to hear our prayers and to grant our petitions:

If my people, which are called by my name, shall humble them- selves, and pray, and seek my face, and turn from their wicked ways; then will I hear from heaven, and will forgive their sin, and will heal their land.   2 Chronicles 7:14

"If my people which are called by my name ... " First, we need to be His people. In other words, we need to have been born into the Kingdom of God. We need to be children of God, restored into fellowship with Him. Then we can call on His name.

Secondly, *"shall humble themselves."* We need to humble our-selves before God. Pride is an abomination before the Lord. When you take things upon yourself, you are proud. When you are not trusting God, you are proud. When you say, "I can do it myself; I don't really need God's help for this," you are proud. If we are to seek His face, we must do it from a position of humility. We must empty ourselves of ourselves if we are to be filled with Him.

Third, *"turn from their wicked ways."* If we want God to heed our prayers, we must depart from evil. We must turn from our sin in repentance. It is safe to say that one prayer God delights in is that of true repentance. He longs to grant our petition when we pray from a pure heart, repenting of our sins. Then God will hear from Heaven and answer our prayer:

> *And ye shall seek me, and find me, when ye shall search for me with all your heart.*   Jeremiah 29:13

We have looked at this verse already, and have seen that when we seek God, we will find Him. But there is something else here that is also important: *"when ye shall search for me with all your heart."* When you pray, when you worship, when you enter into communion with the Lord, it must come from the depths of your heart. These things are not to be religious rituals, words without meaning. Hypocrisy is an abomination before God. Pretension is a sin before the Lord. Let us be people of honesty, of sincerity, of purity, of righteousness before God. Then our prayer will be answered by the Lord:

Therefore I say unto you, What things soever ye desire, when ye pray, believe that ye receive them, and ye shall have them.

Mark 11:24

But without faith it is impossible to please him: for he that cometh to God must believe that he is, and that he is a rewarder of them that diligently seek him. Hebrews 11:6

When we pray, we need to believe. We also need to expect an answer from the Lord. And we need to receive that answer. Believing isn't enough; we need to act on our believing. When we pray, we need to believe, and after believing, we need to visualize that for which we have prayed and believed. After visualizing it, we need to act on it. *"Faith without works is dead"* (James 2:26). When you know what God has promised, you are free to begin to act on that word. Don't continue in misery and in defeat. Act on your prayer. Begin to rejoice and to move in faith. Visualize the victory, the provision, the blessing. Then begin to move in God.

The next verse of the passage is Mark 11 shows us another condition of prayer:

And when ye stand praying, forgive, if ye have ought against any: that your Father also which is in heaven may forgive you your trespasses. But if ye do not forgive, neither will your Father which is in heaven forgive your trespasses. Mark 11:25-26

We need to forgive those who have sinned against us, and this places us in a position to receive God's forgiveness for our own sins. How can He forgive us if we will not forgive others? Don't be fooled; God may sympathize with you, but He will not be convinced that your unforgiveness of others is right. It is a sin against the grace of God.

Christ taught His disciples this principle when He taught them to pray:

> *And forgive us our debts, as we forgive our debtors.*
>
> Matthew 6:12

If you harbor resentment, anger, or animosity in your heart, it will hinder your prayers. Surrender all sin and put it in the hand of God:

> *And whatsoever we ask, we receive of him, because we keep his commandments, and do those things that are pleasing in his sight.* 1 John 3:22

It isn't enough to keep God's commandments; we must also do those things that are pleasing in His sight. Sometimes we do things to please man. But what does it matter if man is pleased with you if you don't have the favor of the Lord?

> *If ye abide in me, and my words abide in you, ye shall ask what ye will, and it shall be done unto you.* John 15:7

Finally, we must abide in Him. We must continue in Christ, remain in Him, be faithful and steadfast in Him. I pray that God will stir your heart to seek Him today.

CHAPTER 7

GOD'S VISION FOR WORSHIP

*O come, let us worship and bow down: let us kneel before the
LORD our maker. For he is our God; and we are the people of his
pasture, and the sheep of his hand.*   Psalm 95:6-7

I believe God wants His Church to be a soul-winning Church;
He wants us to reach out to the lost and to draw them in to the
life of the Lord Jesus. God wants His people to be a praying
people; He wants us to reach out to Him in prayer, communing
and fellowshipping with Him in the Spirit. But there is also
a third element that God has for us. When this aspect of our
spiritual lives is not functioning, then our evangelism becomes
mere good works, and our prayer tends to ritual. This element
of the Christian life is what brings joy. It is what breathes life.
It is what characterizes the vital Christian life. This element is
worship.

It is a privilege to worship the Lord. It is an honor that we are
counted worthy to praise His name. If you are part of a local con-
gregation that regularly enters into times of pure, holy worship,
then you are blessed indeed. It is a joy to come into the House
of the Lord, to come into the sanctuary of God, to enter into the
presence of Christ. The Psalms are filled, not only with expressions
of worship and praise, but also with references to the experience
of entering into worship:

Enter into his gates with thanksgiving, and into his courts with praise: be thankful unto him, and bless his name. For the Lord is good; his mercy is everlasting; and his truth endureth to all generations. Psalm 100:4-5

A Song of degrees of David. I was glad when they said unto me, Let us go into the house of the Lord. Our feet shall stand within thy gates, O Jerusalem. Psalm 122:1

Beloved, let's open our hearts before the Lord and allow Him to teach us how to truly worship.

In John 4, we read the account of Christ's conversation with the Samaritan woman at the well. They had met there by divine appointment. What seemed to have begun as a simple request for a drink of water became a discussion of worship and of the living water that Christ offers. He explained this water to the woman:

Whosoever drinketh of the water that I shall give him shall never thirst; but the water that I shall give him shall be in him a well of water springing up into everlasting life.
The woman saith unto him, Sir, give me this water, that I thirst not, neither come hither to draw. John 4:14-15

There is a well within you that springs up unto life! There is an experience of salvation, of deliverance, of forgiveness of sin that you can know:

There is therefore now no condemnation to them which are in Christ Jesus, who walk not after the flesh, but after the Spirit. Romans 8:1

Therefore being justified by faith, we have peace with God through our Lord Jesus Christ: By whom also we have access by faith into this grace wherein we stand, and rejoice in hope of the glory of God. Romans 5:1-2

This well of living water does not spring up within you just for your own use. It is not there only for you to enjoy. We are not to keep to ourselves the blessings of the Lord. That wellspring is also to flow forth from you:

In the last day, that great day of the feast, Jesus stood and cried, saying, If any man thirst, let him come unto me, and drink. He that believeth on me, as the scripture hath said, out of his belly shall flow rivers of living water. John 7:37-38

Let the waters flow! There is to be a release of the blessing of the Lord into your life so that it can flow forth from you to touch others. Don't try to control or suppress the life of Christ in you. Let it flow forth, for that life within is your only hope of glory!

There is a spiritual reservoir within your heart and spirit. That reservoir is not filled with stagnant water, for there is nothing stagnant about God! It is filled with living water, the water of life that is bubbling up from within. This water of life seeks to be released and to overflow in worship to God.

This wellspring is within your inmost being. Be still. Can you hear that river within you that is roaring with a voice of worship and of praise to our God? Hear that voice that cries out, "Abba, Father!" There is a spirit crying from within that is trying to be released, trying to be set free in the realm of worship.

Release your spirit! Be free in the presence of God! Worship the Lord! Let that river of life within you flow freely. Perhaps you need to help the river along. Is there anything within your life that hinders the flow of Christ's life and of worship? Sometimes there is sin. Sometimes it is bitterness or wrong attitudes. It may be a preoccupation with the busyness of life. Perhaps it is concern over what others will think of you. Look within to find any debris that hinders the flow. Then clear it away. Pray and release those things to God. Repent of any sin. Allow the Lord to wash you clean, that His river may flow in you unpolluted.

What does this have to do with worship? Everything! I believe that worship is the overflow of the life of Christ within. Worship flows freely as we recognize the way of repentance, the power of forgiveness, and the joy of coming to a place of absolute surrender to God. Worship flows when we allow the Holy Spirit to unshackle us from every stronghold that the enemy has set up in our lives.

Why do we sometimes grumble, murmur, and complain? I believe it is because the life of Christ is diminishing instead of increasing within us. And our complaining hastens the process. We must become more like John the Baptist, who said, *"He must increase, but I must decrease"* (John 3:30).

Worship feeds on itself. The more you enter into a spirit of worship, the more that spirit is stirred within you, and the more you will want to worship and draw close to your Lord. Worship brings you into a position of growing in the knowledge of the truth and of God's power. It brings you into a place of freedom and liberty in God. Worship places you in a position of rejoicing in the presence of God. So let your worship overflow. Don't hold it in. Express it to the Lord.

As a glass that is filled to overflowing, so are you in the hand of God. He is continually pouring forth of His life, His love, His presence, His Spirit into your life. As long as you remain open to Him, you are filled and saturated with this water of life. There is nothing you can do to stop this flow or to contain it. You have no choice but to allow this water to flood your life with worship.

As this happens, your thoughts begin to change. No longer are you dwelling on negative thoughts, consumed only with the cares of everyday life. No longer is that deadline quite so dreaded, that boss quite so difficult to handle, those bills quite so overpowering. Instead, you begin to think about the goodness, the faithfulness, and the forgiveness of the Lord. You begin to meditate on the ministry of the Lord. You begin to ponder in your heart the graciousness and the kindness of God.

But such thoughts cannot be contained inside! As you think on these things, you will begin to rejoice and be happy in the Lord. That's when worship becomes a reality to you.

Beloved, worship is not a religious ritual, nor is it a doctrine that can be taught and understood. It is a blessing, an opportunity that God has given to us that we may enter into His presence. It is the way by which we may have an intimate communion and relationship with Him. It is only through worship that we are finally released from every tradition, every religiosity, every cultural mindset, every barrier, until we see nothing except the glory, the presence, the power, and the magnitude of God's presence moving, flowing, and working in our lives.

I need to clarify something. Very often we tend to divide praise and worship. In many churches there seems to be an understanding that praise consists of singing lively songs, swaying in time with the music, or dancing, beating the drums, pounding the piano or the organ, ans playing fast licks on the guitar. We tend to think of praise in terms of making a joyful noise unto the Lord. Then we slow things down. We sing solemn songs accompanied by soft music and think that we are entering into worship.

In reality, there is very little difference between worship and praise. The two go hand in hand. You cannot worship without praising God, and you cannot praise God without worshiping Him. Each is a privilege. So what is the difference between the two?

Praise is a response to the benefits and the blessings you have received; it flows forth because of what the Lord has done for you. God has done some wonderful things! He answers our prayers. He saves us and our loved ones. He heals our bodies. He provides for us. He allows us to sense His presence. The Lord continually performs wonderful works of grace, which cause the praise to well up within His people. When you see the creation of God and the wonders of His works, your natural response is to praise Him. Praise has a point of origin.

Let's imagine you were to give someone a gift. Suppose the recipient opens the package and says, "Oh, is that all it is?" and then lays it aside. That would be an insult to the giver. Or perhaps he might say, "It's okay, brother. That's all right, sister. It's the thought that counts." That's even worse! But maybe he will say, "Ah, thank you! You didn't need to do this, but out of the kindness and goodness of your heart, you expressed your love to me. Thank you!" The recipient begins to praise and to rejoice because there is a benefit that he has received. This is praise.

Worship is totally different. Worship is not based on what you have received or on what God has done for you. It is not the result of anything God has given you. Instead, worship comes from the depths of your spirit when you begin to recognize who God is. He is not only the Blesser; He is God Almighty. We worship Him, not because of what He has given us, but because of who He is. Thus we can worship Him in spite of the fact that we are not blessed, in spite of the fact that we are not yet healed, in spite of the fact that our problems are still current and our situation has not yet changed. In spite of all these things, we can still worship God. Why? Because He's God.

It's not difficult to praise the Lord when all your bills are paid and you have extra money. It isn't hard to praise Him when you are healthy and your body is feeling great. It's easy to praise Him when your situation is pleasant. But it's more difficult to praise God when your pockets are empty and you have nothing to eat. It's hard to praise Him when your electricity or telephone service might be cut off. And it's not easy to praise Him from a bed of pain.

Can you still worship the Lord when things are difficult? Too often we look to the gift rather than to the Giver. We focus on the need rather than on the One who can meet the need. But we are to look to God in all things, in both good times and bad. He is ever worthy, regardless of our circumstances.

Worship is a powerful thing. It can change our perspective, even when our situation is not changed. In looking to God, we are changed:

Beloved, now are we the sons of God, and it doth not yet appear what we shall be: but we know that, when he shall appear, we shall be like him; for we shall see him as he is. 1 John 3:2

Praise and worship are not optional. They are not to be practiced only when things are going well for us, only when we feel like it, or only when we are meeting together with the Church for times of corporate praise:

> *Sing unto the LORD, all the earth; show forth from day to day his salvation. Declare his glory among the heathen; his marvellous works among all nations. For great is the LORD, and greatly to be praised: he also is to be feared above all gods. For all the gods of the people are idols: but the LORD made the heavens. Glory and honour are in his presence; strength and gladness are in his place.* 1 Chronicles 16:23-27

We are to *"show forth"* His salvation day after day. In other words, those around us should be able to see it. It should be evident in our actions, our words, our attitudes, our relations with others, that we know God and His salvation. So, rejoice in the Lord! Be happy in Him. Show forth the joy of your salvation.

This psalm also instructs us to declare God's glory among the heathen, or the nations. We are to proclaim His glory. We should be living, walking advertisements for the glory of the Lord, speaking of His wonderful deeds. *"For great is the LORD, and greatly to be praised."* Amen! He is worthy of all our praise, adoration, thanksgiving, and worship.

As the psalmist meditated on the attributes of the Lord, he came to see that He is surrounded with glory and honor, strength, and gladness. God is infinite, absolute, and glorious beyond description. There is no imperfection in Him. He cannot be explained or described. Our human minds cannot comprehend the immensity or the intensity of the vastness and the greatness of His glory and power. God dwells in glory, splendor, and majesty.

Since we are the dwelling place of God, His strength and joy abide in us. Each time we worship, each time we extol God, each time we magnify Him, we are building Him a dwelling place. The Bible tells us that God inhabits—He dwells, abides, resides, lives in—the praises of His people (see Psalm 22:3.)

Many scriptures speak of the joys and blessings of knowing the Lord:

For in him we live, and move, and have our being; as certain also of your own poets have said, for we are also his offspring.

Acts 17:28

Thou wilt show me the path of life: in thy presence is fulness of joy; at thy right hand there are pleasures for evermore.

Psalm 16:11

Neither be ye sorry; for the joy of the Lord is your strength.

Nehemiah 8:10b

As we have read, *"Strength and gladness are in his place"* (1 Chronicles 16:27). But often, instead of being joyful, we are discontented. Instead of our hearts being filled with praise and worship to our God, we are filled with complaints. We murmur, we criticize, we find fault, and we sit in judgment, looking down upon our brothers and sisters because they are not just like us.

When we look to our God, this all starts to change. Worship will change your attitudes, even if the problem is still there. Worship will change your focus, It will change you. If you give yourself to worshiping the Lord, you will be transformed from a complainer to a worshiper, from one who murmurs to one who gives thanks. Rather than looking at your problems, you will be looking to your Lord. As you look to Jesus, the Author and the Finisher of our faith, as you gaze into His face, you will rise up in the glory of God.

Isaiah experienced this, and described it for us:

> *In the year that king Uzziah died I saw also the* LORD *sitting upon a throne, high and lifted up, and his train filled the temple. Above it stood the seraphims: each one had six wings; with twain he covered his face, and with twain he covered his feet, and with twain he did fly. And one cried unto another, and said, Holy, holy, holy, is the* LORD *of hosts: the whole earth is full of his glory.*
>
> Isaiah 6:1-3

When Isaiah looked to the Lord, when his eyes were opened to the surpassing glory of God, he could truly say that the whole earth is full of His glory. Were there no longer any problems in the world or in Isaiah's personal life? Of course there were. But Isaiah had his eyes fixed upon the Lord in His glory, and all else faded away.

Turn your eyes upon Jesus
Look full in His wonderful face
And the things of earth
Will grow strangely dim
In the light of His glory and grace[1]

---

1. *Turn Your Eyes Upon Jesus* by Helen H. Lemmel

As we look to the Lord, our worries and cares will take on their proper perspective and appearance; for when we magnify the Lord, He increases, and all else decreases:

Ascribe to the Lord, O families of nations, ascribe to the Lord glory and strength, ascribe to the Lord the glory due his name. Bring an offering and come before him; worship the Lord in the splendor of his holiness. Tremble before him, all the earth! The world is firmly established; it cannot be moved. Let the heavens rejoice, let the earth be glad; let them say among the nations, "The Lord reigns!" Let the sea resound, and all that is in it; let the fields be jubilant, and everything in them! Then the trees of the forest will sing, they will sing for joy before the Lord, for he comes to judge the earth. 1 Chronicles 16:28-33, NIV

All of God's creation worships Him! The fields are jubilant, and the trees sing. This reminds me of Christ's words as recorded in the gospel of Luke:

And he [Jesus] answered and said unto them, I tell you that, if these [children] should hold their peace, the stones would immediately cry out. Luke 19:40

The rocks and the trees, the fields and the seas, all join in praising God. I have a question for you: will you let the trees take your place? I won't! I will worship the Lord:

Save us, O Lord our God, and gather us from among the heathen, to give thanks unto thy holy name, and to triumph in thy praise.

*Blessed be the L*ORD *God of Israel from everlasting to everlasting: and let all the people say, Amen. Praise ye the L*ORD.

Psalm 106:47-48

Praise is not an alternative; it is a requirement for us. Like it or not, you need to praise God. We praise and worship Him for what He has done, we praise and worship Him for what He is doing right now, and we praise and worship Him for what He promised He will do.

You need to worship God. You really have no other choice. Why is that? Is it because God has such a huge ego? No! It is because it is only by taking our eyes off of ourselves and our circumstances that we can rise above them. It is only by looking to Jesus that we can know peace and healing. Any other "solution" is a temporary help at best.

If you lay aside your difficulties long enough to worship the Lord when things seem to be at their worst, then you will find that they no longer seem to be quite so bad. It is not that God will automatically change your circumstances; but your perspective will be different:

Humble yourselves in the sight of the Lord, and he shall lift you up. James 4:10

If you will humble yourself, laying aside the concerns of self and pouring yourself out in worship before the Lord, then He will lift you up. He will elevate you to a new position in the spiritual realms, and from that new place, you will look at life differently:

But God, who is rich in mercy, for his great love wherewith he loved us, even when we were dead in sins, hath quickened us together with Christ, (by grace ye are saved;) and hath raised us up together, and made us sit together in heavenly places in Christ Jesus: that in the ages to come he might show the exceeding riches of his grace in his kindness toward us through Christ Jesus. Ephesians 2:4-7

As we look to the Lord in worship, we are able to enter into and experience the reality of which this passage speaks. God has raised us up to sit in heavenly places in Christ; but the sad truth is that most of the time we don't really live this way. What we think of as reality—the situations and problems we face daily—inhibits our ability to see true reality, which is the truth proclaimed in God's Word. Worship allows us to clear our vision so that we become God-conscious and God-focused.

The Scriptures contain many invitations to worship. We are encouraged to enter into this special relationship with God.

O come, let us sing unto the Lord: let us make a joyful noise to the rock of our salvation. Psalm 95:1

O magnify the Lord with me, and let us exalt his name together. Psalm 34:3

I was glad when they said unto me, Let us go into the house of the Lord. Psalm 122:1

"Let us go into the house of the Lord." Let us go into the presence of God. Let us bring our petition to the Lord, and let us cast our

burdens upon Him. Let us cry unto God, for He will hear us. Let us come before the Lord. Let us run after Him. Come, and let us sing for joy to the Lord! He is inviting you. Will you come?

Beloved, worship does not always flow naturally from our inward man. Sometimes we must be determined to rise out of our unpleasant circumstances and lift our spirits in worship. Sometimes it takes a conscious decision of the will for us to enter into worship.

Let us not be silent! Do not be afraid to enter into the presence of the Lord. Do not be afraid to lose yourself in praise. Sometimes others will not understand you when you are worshiping the Lord, but that's all right. God is looking to your heart, not your approval ratings. When we come under the anointing of the Lord, we lose our sophistication, our sense of reserve. Instead, we are energized and quickened by the Spirit of God. When we are released into the presence of God, we act differently. We lift up our voices in song, we shout, we cry, and we laugh as the joy of the Lord fills our souls.

When we are founded upon the Rock, Christ Jesus, the storms of life lose their terror. Jesus spoke of the wise man who built his house upon the rock and the foolish man who built his house upon the sand (see Matthew 7:24-27). Regardless of where you build, one thing is sure: the storms will come.

Storms will come, and storms will disappear. Shaking will come, and the shaking will end. In all situations, if you are grounded in the Lord Jesus Christ, all you can say is:

Bless the Lord, O my soul: and all that is within me, bless his holy name.   Psalm 103:1

Worship will bring you to a place of victory and deliverance, a place of security and the provision of God. Worship will bring you to the freedom of the Lord and to satisfaction and contentment in Him. As you enter into worship, the glory of the Lord will overflow you, and God will reveal His power.

Paul and Silas experienced this. They had been beaten and thrown into jail. Their crime? They had cast a spirit of divination out of a slave girl. They could have despaired, but they made a decision to enter into worship and praise, even in the midst of their pain and surroundings:

> *And at midnight Paul and Silas prayed, and sang praises unto God: and the prisoners heard them. And suddenly there was a great earthquake, so that the foundations of the prison were shaken: and immediately all the doors were opened, and every one's bands were loosed.*　　　　　Acts 16:25-26

As Paul and Silas began to worship God, He manifested His power and His glory inside that prison. God began to join with them in singing, so that it rocked the jail. The chains that were binding them were broken, the doors were opened, and the prisoners set free—all because worship had brought those two believers into a higher realm in God.

But do you know what I think? Even if those doors had not been shaken open, even if those chains had held fast, Paul and Silas would have kept right on praising God.

Beloved, it is wonderful when we sense God's presence. It is beautiful when we receive the blessing of the Lord and know that His hand is upon us for good. But we need to learn to worship when blessings come and also when they don't. Our worship doesn't depend upon receiving God's blessing. Our worship depends on our understanding of who God is.

No matter what my circumstances are, the Lord is still my Savior. He is yet the Lover of my soul. He remains my All in All through every situation, the good and the bad. If you are in a time of difficulty, then take your eyes off of your problems. Look to God and say to yourself, "It doesn't matter what will happen. What I need to do is to rejoice in the Lord. I need to recognize that He is God and He alone is worthy of praise and worship. I will worship Him, and I will adore Him." Then do it! You will experience the release that comes to us when we focus our spirits upon the Lord God instead of on the difficulties that surround us.

It is a joy to know the love of God and receive forgiveness of sin through our Lord Jesus Christ.

It is a blessing to experience God's awesome presence, power and greatness. It is a comfort and great encouragement to know that with God all things are possible. It is an honor and privilege to be intimate with God in worship. It is a blessing to walk with God, who promised never to leave or forsake me but will be with me till the end. It gives me so much peace and joy to know that God cares for me and is watching over me both night and day. What a joy and privilege it is for me to live for Him and serve Him all the days of my life. I have decided to follow Jesus. No turning back. No turning back.

Your faith will blossom as you praise Him, recounting the good things He has done in your life so far, and releasing Him to bless you even more.

CHAPTER 8

THE VISION FOR WORSHIP BECOMES OUR MISSION

Thou shalt have no other gods before me.   Exodus 20:3

I believe this is the most crucial of the Ten Commandments. In fact, all the others hinge on this one command. Think about it. If you treasure material things over your walk with God, you won't mind coveting or stealing. If you prize doing as you wish at all times, then you won't necessarily remember to keep the Sabbath holy. If you find someone's charms of greater appeal than God's call to righteous living, you might not be concerned about what God has to say about adultery. If we put God first, the rest will follow.

Much of the Church today seems to have lost sight of this command and of this principle. Look around you, and what do you see? Christians who look like the world, who dress like the world, who talk like the world, and who act like the world. There's just one problem with this: we are not of this world, so we have no business following after society's trends and dictates, not when we claim to know the true and living God.

The sad part of all of this is that many believers don't even realize they are following the world's ways. Worse, they don't recognize that they have gone into idolatry.

There are other, more subtle, kinds of idolatry as well. For instance, how attached are you to your local church's way of worship? If you visit another church whose members worship differently, can you enter into worship? Our expressions of worship, even if they began as beautiful ways to express our adoration to the Lord, can turn into idolatry. Do you have a favorite Bible teacher whose messages you never miss? This, too, can turn to idolatry. We must guard our hearts well, since all of us are prone to sin.

Too often, when we think of idolatry, we think in Old Testament terms. We think of Baal or of Molech. But we don't seem to understand that idolatry is alive and well and flourishing even in the church.

Worship is a gift that God has given us. It is a blessing, and an expression of devotion and communion with God. Our worship should be given only to the Lord God. No one else is worthy to be worshiped and adored. God alone is the One who is *"high and lifted up."* We are to look up to Him. Too often we look up to people. We look up to the icons of Hollywood or Broadway, to those in government or in fashion. We look up to the world when we have every reason to look higher still.

Our worship—all of our worship—must be directed toward God. If you miss a church service to stay home and watch television, then you are worshiping the TV set. If you are missing church to sleep in, then you are worshiping the bed. If God is directing you to a time of prayer but you decide to go shopping, you are worshiping your own way and the material goods you are seeking. Anything that is more important to you than God and your relationship with Him is an idol to you.

What does God's Word say? *"Thou shalt love the* LORD *thy God with all thy heart."* Many people stop there, but that is not all there is to that verse. Jesus said it this way:

And thou shalt love the Lord *thy God with all thy heart, and with all thy soul, and with all thy mind, and with all thy strength: this is the first commandment.* Mark 12:30

Loving God on a soulish, emotional level is not enough. We need to study and search the Scriptures, delighting ourselves in them. We need to ponder the questions of faith and doubt that arise, looking to the Word by the Spirit to find our answers. We need to use our minds in our walk with God, for we are to love Him with our minds. We must strive in our relationship with the Lord, allowing Him to test our commitment to Him as He did so often throughout scripture with those who would be found faithful. We must love Him with all the strength of our will, our emotions, our minds, our physical bodies, our spirits. There is much more to expressing our love to the Lord—which is what worship is really all about—than singing a few songs in church. The psalmist cried out:

Bless the Lord, *O my soul: and all that is within me, bless his holy name.* Psalm 103:1

Let us worship the Lord with all of who we are, for He is worthy of such adoration. And let us worship Him alone, and none other:

Sing unto the Lord, *all the earth; show forth from day to day his salvation. Declare his glory among the heathen; his marvellous works among all nations. For great is the* Lord, *and greatly to be praised: he also is to be feared above all gods. For all the gods of the people are idols: but the* Lord *made the heavens. Glory and honour are in his presence; strength and gladness are in his place.*   1 Chronicles 26:23-27

Is there anyone else who can compare with the greatness of our God? Is there anyone else who could possibly surpass the vastness of His majestic power? No! *"For great is the Lord and most worthy of praise."* There may be idols, but there is none that can compare with the Lord our God. He is worthy of all worship and all praise.

You are beautiful beyond description,
Too marvellous for words,
Too wonderful for comprehension,
Like nothing ever seen or heard.
Who can grasp your infinite wisdom?
Who can fathom the depth of your love?
You are beautiful beyond description,
Majesty enthroned above.[1]

The song on 1 Chronicles 26 continues:

Give unto the Lord, *ye kindreds of the people, give unto the* Lord *glory and strength. Give unto the* Lord *the glory due unto his name: bring an offering, and come before him: worship the* Lord *in the beauty of holiness. Fear before him, all the earth: the world also shall be stable, that it be not moved. Let the heavens be glad, and let the earth rejoice: and let men say among the nations, The* Lord *reigneth.*   1 Chronicles 26:28-31

1. *I Stand in Awe of You* by Mark Altrogge

The Lord reigns! Heaven and earth shall proclaim it with joy and rejoicing. What a beautiful picture of worship! According to the following verses, even the fields and the trees worship the Lord, all of creation unites to exalt the Creator. And how should we worship Him? In the beauty of our good works, or our good intentions? No, we are to worship in the beauty of holiness. There should be nothing between God and us, no other loves that would interfere in our relationship with Him.

The book of Psalms contains many beautiful passages of praise and worship to God. The Psalm 95 is one of encouragement and exhortation, written by one with a heart to see others enter into worship:

> *O come, let us sing unto the LORD: let us make a joyful noise to the rock of our salvation. Let us come before his presence with thanksgiving, and make a joyful noise unto him with psalms. For the LORD is a great God, and a great King above all gods.*
>
> Psalm 95:1-3

The writer invites you: *"Come."* "Celebrate in the presence of the Lord," says the psalmist. "Let us worship Him together. *Come!"*

It doesn't matter how you happen to feel at the moment. It doesn't matter what your circumstances may be. The invitation is the same at all times: "Come, and let us worship the Lord." The reason is also the same always: *"For the Lord is a great God."*

Lord, you are
More precious than silver.
Lord, you are
More costly than gold.

Lord, you are
More beautiful than diamonds,
And nothing I desire
Compares with you.[2]

Our God is awesome. He is indescribable. No language of the human tongue can describe the infinite greatness of His majestic power and glory. There is nothing that can begin to describe Him ... except worship. Worship is the only thing that can at least begin to touch upon who God is. Such worship comes, not from the mind, not from the soul, and not from the body; but such worship springs forth from within the spirit, for it is the spirit of man that worships God:

> *But the hour cometh, and now is, when the true worshippers shall worship the Father in spirit and in truth: for the Father seeketh such to worship him. God is a Spirit: and they that worship him must worship him in spirit and in truth.*   John 4:23-24

God is looking for those who will worship Him *"in spirit and in truth."* He takes worship seriously, and so should we.

In case we have not yet gotten the message, Psalm 95 continues with another invitation to worship:

> *O come, let us worship and bow down: let us kneel before the* LORD *our maker.*   Psalm 95:6

We are invited to bow down, to kneel before the Lord. In times past, when kings or queens, princes or princesses, emperors or

2. By Oasis Worship and Randy Rothwell

governors or anyone else who was in a position of high authority passed by, what did all the subjects do? They bowed down. Failure to bow before a king or ruler could mean death. Bowing was a mark of respect, not only for the ruler himself, but also for the power that particular leader wielded. How much more should we bow before our King, in respect and honor both for Him and for the awesome power which is His!

Sadly, when we come into the presence of the Lord, we begin to shout, saying things like this: "God, You promised You'd do this! I'm still waiting for You! Lord, if You're not going to do it now, You'll be sorry!"

We cannot stand in the presence of God in self-righteousness or in our own goodness. The very best we have to offer is still as filthy rags in the sight of God. We need to bow down when we come to worship the Lord, recognizing who He is. We need to submit to His authority, surrender to His control, and acknowledge His supremacy and His government over our lives.

When we bow before Him, may it be in the brokenness of our hearts and the contriteness of our spirits, and may we worship Him from the depths of our hearts. Then will we be transformed, cleansed by the blood of Jesus Christ, and released from condemnation and from every guilt. We will stand in the righteousness of Jesus Christ.

Know this:

There are no problems so great that God cannot solve them.
There no needs so great that God cannot provide them.
There are no shackles so powerful that God cannot break them.
There is no darkness that the glory of God cannot brighten.
There are armies so powerful that God cannot conquer them

There are no burdens so heavy that God cannot lift them. There are no scars so deep that God cannot erase them.

It is this comprehension of who He is that stimulates praise in our hearts. And that praise brings us to a sense of awe and of worship.

There's a very fine line between praise and worship. When you are worshiping God, you are praising Him. When you are praising God, you are worshiping Him. Worship and praise should be approached as one act, for they are closely intertwined. And both should be given to God.

How can we hold anything closer in our hearts than God? Think of the wonders of His creation, His majestic handiwork. Consider those times when your needs have been met or when your sicknesses and infirmities have been healed. These are the things for which we praise God. Can a new house do these things? Can clothes, or cars, or books, or anything else that we might hold dear to our hearts, do this? Of course not! Praise flows forth from our hearts to God because of the things He has done.

When we meditate on the kindness, the provision, and the mercy demonstrated to us by God, praise, thanks, and adoration is our normal response. How can we not thank Him for His deep compassion for us? How can we not praise God for His mercy to us or adore Him for His love for us? These things all fall into the realm of praise.

But we don't need to wait for a blessing before we worship God. We don't need to wait for a special kindness, for a healing, or for a financial blessing. We don't worship Him on the basis of what He has given us or what He has promised us, but on the basis of who He is. We worship Him in spite of the fact that we are sick, in spite of the fact that we see no way for our bills to be paid, in spite of the fact that a spouse has walked away from the relationship.

Worship does not depend on what God has done for us lately. We worship God because of who He is. Even if I am not blessed, even if I am not healed, even if my husband or my wife will not reconcile with me, even if my own children turn their backs on me and on my God, I can still worship Him because of who He is.

God is a Giver, and it is difficult to separate who He is from His gifts, difficult to separate His personality, His character, His person from the blessings we have received from Him. When we are in relationship with God, there will be blessing, there will be promises, there will be prosperity, healing, and many other good things. But our relationship with God should not be established on our receiving or on His giving.

God is not Santa Claus. No matter what you have or what you don't have, God is worthy to be worshiped because He is God.

Let's take this a step further. Why do you worship the Lord? Worship is to be a time when you pour yourself out, giving of yourself to God. Many of us look forward to receiving in worship and judge whether a time of worship was "good" or not by whether we sensed the presence of the Lord. But this should not be!

Worship is a pouring out, not a taking in. If we judge our worship at all (and is this not something for God to judge?), then it should be by the measure of how much of ourselves we have poured out to Him. Too often, we look for those good, positive feelings that we associate with "sensing the presence of the Lord." In reality, if we were truly experiencing His presence, I believe there would be more times of corporate repentance, more seasons of solitary prayer, and far less sin in the church.

Isaiah once entered into a time of vision. He saw the Lord God, lofty and majestic. He saw the angelic beings and heard their worship. He really felt the presence of the Lord at that meeting! And what was his response?

> *Then said I, Woe is me! for I am undone; because I am a man of unclean lips, and I dwell in the midst of a people of unclean lips: for mine eyes have seen the King, the* LORD *of hosts.* Isaiah 6:5

Isaiah saw the Lord, and as a result, he was made painfully conscious of his own sin. Experiencing God's presence is not always the warm and wonderful thing that we have made it out to be. When these times come, be they times of joy or times of repentance, it is good, but let us not look to them to determine the acceptance of our worship. Let us worship the Lord because He is worthy and only because He is worthy!

In an earlier chapter, I said that prayer is the breath of the spirit, the life of the spirit, and when prayer ceases, so does the life of the spirit. But worship is the spirit's song. As music can be an expression of the deep stirrings of the soul, so can worship express the deep things of the spirit. Prayer and worship walk hand in hand in our lives, teaching us to know and to love our Lord.

It is sometimes difficult to communicate concerning worship, since it is a very personal act. We each bring our ideas of what constitutes worship into any discussion of the subject. So let's look to the Word of God for help in understanding what worship really is or should be. There are several Hebrew and Greek words translated as *worship* in our Bibles. We will look at three of these Greek words.

The first of these words is *proskunew.* This is a rich word which embodies several meanings: "to kiss the hand toward someone as a token of reverence, to kneel or prostrate oneself in order to do homage to another, to bow, either to show respect or to make a request." This word implies humility and submission.

This is the word for worship in these passages, among others:

Now when Jesus was born in Bethlehem of Judaea in the days of Herod the king, behold, there came wise men from the east to Jerusalem, saying, Where is he that is born King of the Jews? for we have seen his star in the east, and are come to worship him.
Matthew 2:1-2

When he was come down from the mountain, great multitudes followed him. And, behold, there came a leper and worshipped him, saying, Lord, if thou wilt, thou canst make me clean.
Matthew 8:1-2

While he spake these things unto them, behold, there came a certain ruler, and worshipped him, saying, My daughter is even now dead: but come and lay thy hand upon her, and she shall live. And Jesus arose, and followed him, and so did his disciples.
Matthew 9:18-19

[After Jesus had walked upon the water and then entered

the disciples' boat], *then they that were in the ship came and worshipped him, saying, Of a truth thou art the Son of God.*

Matthew 14:33

These are just a few examples of the use of *proskunew*. It is used in describing magi awed by the newborn King. It speaks of the heart of the leper when faced with the Person of his only hope for healing, and of the hope of the distraught father who places his trust in Jesus. It speaks of the awe of ordinary men who had just witnessed a most extraordinary action on the part of the One they called Friend.

It is used in other places as well: describing the actions of the Gentile woman with the demon-possessed child; describing the response of the man born deaf when at last he found his Healer; describing the response of the disciples to the appearance of the risen Lord.

Have you seen God at work in your life? Do you have a sense of awe when you think of Christ's blood being shed for you, of His salvation at work within you? Christ is your King! Bow down before Him in humility, knowing that it is His righteousness and not your own that gives you access to the Father.

You cannot worship God with a proud heart or a rebellious spirit. Bowing down to the ground is a humbling experience, because it physically lowers you. Our natural desire is to be lifted up, exalted, but worship brings us to a place of humility as we look to the One who is worthy to be lifted up.

Worship is not just about humility; it is also about intimacy. *Proskunew* literally means "to kiss toward." Does this describe your worship? Think of the final moments of the wedding ceremony, when the groom is told, "You may kiss the bride." There is joy in that kiss! The bride and groom are not ashamed to kiss one another in front of everyone present. They are proud to have an intimate relationship. They are proud to be together. They are not embarrassed to let everyone know that they have such a relationship.

Worship is expressing your love and devotion to God. It is literally like kissing Him. Worship brings you so close to God that you become intertwined with Him. Worship breaks all the barriers of culture and tradition to bring you into a place of intimacy and communion with the Lord. When was the last time you embraced God? When was the last time you worshiped God from the depths of your spirit?

God broke down the barriers of eternity past. His Son was stripped of all glory and splendor so that He could come to kiss us, sinful though we are, and restore us to fellowship with Him. Isn't it time that we, His creation, redeemed by the Lord, kissed in worship the One who is the Lover of our soul?

A second Greek word for worship is *sebomai*, which means "to revere or to worship." It implies "awe or devotion." This is the devotion of the dog that follows its beloved master wherever he goes. The dog does not understand the master's motives; sometimes it has no idea what the master is doing. Yet it loyally follows him, not questioning, but trusting. The dog is ready to go wherever the master is going. It is ready to face any discomfort simply for the joy of being with the master. The animal is ever on the alert to do the bidding of the master.

We should have this type of devotion to God. We should be ready to follow wherever He might lead and be looking for any opportunity to do His bidding. Throughout the day, we are to express this type of devotion to God. "What is Your purpose for me today, Lord? What is Your plan for me today?" Your reward will not be found in any gratification of your own self; it will be found in your delight and pleasure in being in the presence of the Master.

The final word I want to look at, although there are more than these three words used in the Greek, is *latreuw*. This word is related to *latris*, which means "a hired menial servant." *Latreuw* means "to serve or minister to, either to God or men." It includes the ideas of "giving homage, of performing religious service, of offering gifts, and of worshiping God by the observance of the rites instituted for His worship."

We are to be servants of the Lord. When you serve God with all your heart, He views it as worship unto Him.

Paul spoke of his service as worship:

> *But this I confess unto thee, that after the way which they call heresy, so worship* [latreuw] *I the God of my fathers, believing all things which are written in the law and in the prophets.*   Acts 24:14

Later, Paul used this same Greek word in speaking to the men aboard the ship that was taking him to Rome. In this account, it is translated as *"serve"*:

> *For there stood by me this night the angel of God, whose I am, and whom I serve.*   Acts 27:23

Worship and service are intertwined for the believer. All that we do in the Kingdom in service to God has the potential to be an expression of worship. It all depends on our motives and on our hearts. Are we doing what we do out of love for the Lord or out of a sense of duty? Are we more compelled by the Spirit that dwells within us or by the expectations of men? Let us give heed to the Word, so that:

> *Whatsoever ye do in word or deed, do all in the name of the* Lord *Jesus, giving thanks to God and the Father by him.*
>
> Colossians 3:17

"Whatsoever ye do ..." If we evangelize the lost, it is worship to God. If we minister to the needy, it is worship to God. If we pray, it is worship to God.

God has a vision for the Church. He wants us to be a people who reach out to the lost. He wants us to be a people of prayer. He wants us to be a people of worship. Let us rise up and become the Church that God wants us to be, the Church that God intends us to be. Let us be the Church that fulfills God's vision for His people! Let His vision become our mission!

AUTHOR CONTACT PAGE

You may contact Bishop Ray Llarena directly at:

Global Evangelistic Ministries
9039 Lakeshore Dr.
Pleasant Prairie, WI 53158

Email: bishopray1@yahoo.com